THE PERFECT CLOSE WORKBOOK

By JAMES MUIR

James Muir

THE PERFECT CLOSE WORKBOOK
© April 2018
By JAMES MUIR

All rights reserved. No part of this book may be reproduced, stored in a retrieval system, or transmitted in any form or by any means, electronic, mechanical, photocopying, recording, scanning, or otherwise, without the prior written permission of the publisher except for the use of brief quotations in a book review.

For permission requests, write to the publisher, addressed "Attention: Permissions Coordinator" at the address below.
Best Practice International
14267 Bailey Hill Way
Herriman, UT 84096
http://www.bestpracticeinternational.com/

Ordering Information:

Quantity sales. Special discounts are available on quantity purchases by corporations, associations, and others. For details, contact the publisher at the address above.

For information visit http://PureMuir.com

Book Cover design by Ivan Terzic

Publisher: Best Practice International

ISBN: 978-1790921799

BISAC: Business & Economics / Sales & Selling / General

1. Business & Economics 2. Sales & Selling 3. General

First Edition: December 2018

Dedicated to the teachable individuals of the world who learn, grow, and share what they learn with others.

Why I Wrote This Book

This workbook is the companion guide to the various Perfect Close workshops. It contains all the supporting models, exercises, forms, reference guides, and resources for those workshops.

Shortly after publishing *The Perfect Close* I discovered that the need for workshops and coaching far outpaced my ability to deliver them. *The Perfect Close* became a best-seller immediately after being published and spent its entire first year in the top-ten sales titles (often in the number one position). I say this not to brag but to illustrate how dissatisfied the world is with the manipulative approaches and closes of yesteryear.

For that reason, I wrote this – *The Perfect Close Workbook* – to allow individuals and organizations to independently work through all the steps to implement and incorporate The Perfect Close concepts and methodology into their organizations.

Everything you need to learn and implement The Perfect Close is contained within these pages. If you were to attend any Perfect Close workshop, this is the workbook we would use. In a workshop environment, in addition to what you see here, we would leverage group activities to enhance learning, but all the models, exercises, forms and reference guides are contained herein and suitable for individual development.

If you invest the short amount of time it takes to learn this clear and simple method, you will dramatically improve your sales results and make all your interactions profoundly more enjoyable.

It is my hope that you will achieve the same level of success and happiness that knowing these things has afforded me.

Table of Contents

Why I Wrote This Book iv

Introduction – How to Get the Most from The Perfect Close Workbook vi

CHAPTER 1 - Why Do You Want to Improve Your Closing Skills? 1

CHAPTER 2 - Sales is Service 9

CHAPTER 3 - Mindset 13

CHAPTER 4 - What Is Closing? 27

CHAPTER 5 - Planning = Success 33

CHAPTER 6 - The Critical Advance 39

CHAPTER 7 - How to Set Call Objectives 49

CHAPTER 8 - Why Should This Client See Me? 55

CHAPTER 9 - What Do I Want My Prospective Client to Do? 63

CHAPTER 10 - How Can I Provide Value on This Encounter? 73

CHAPTER 11 - Planning Sales Encounters 97

CHAPTER 12 - Leveraging Agendas for Effective Sales Encounters 110

CHAPTER 13 - The Perfect Close 121

CHAPTER 14 - Putting It All Together 142

Free Additional Resources 144

Recommended Reading 154

Request For Review 156

About the Author 157

Introduction –
How to Get the Most from
The Perfect Close Workbook

One challenge to learning is the ability to translate general concepts into your own specific situations. I often see that while everyone understands the principles and concepts involved in this book, many find it difficult to apply them (the actual words, activities, phrases, etc.) in their daily sales efforts. Making the concepts real for you is an important part of what *The Perfect Close Workbook* does. It turns the intangible into the tangible. Here's how:

The Perfect Close Workbook is a "work" book. Meaning, it's designed to be used actively as you read it. To get the most from it, write in it and refer to it often. The greatest value of the book is not in its words and instructions but rather in the words that *you* write in it, and the discovery and growth that occurs as you complete the exercises.

Actually do all the exercises—just looking at them will not help you sell better. It is while you read, contemplate, and complete each exercise that your knowledge and understanding will expand, and the habits formed from completing the exercises will become naturally available to you in your daily activities. These are the frameworks and tools to help you sell successfully. So, complete the exercises and reap the value of this workbook.

Also, take advantage of FREE additional resources available exclusively to you and other purchasers at PureMuir.com/TPCworkbook. Find your online access password in the Free Additional Resources section in the back of this book.

That said, pace yourself as you go through all the material. If you read this book in a single day, you'll likely fail to incorporate all the concepts into your daily routine. Take your time to learn, discover, and apply the principles. There's no need to race to the end. I can tell you the conclusion right now: by methodically working through these exercises you will achieve a measurable improvement in your selling and in your enjoyment of selling.

And, the potential to improve your life is dramatic. Not only have the concepts of this book made a big and lasting impact on my life, it has done the same for many others. Just this morning, as I write this, I received an email with the following comment, "James, your book [*The Perfect Close*] has changed my life, at work, with friends, and even with my wife... yes some of your philosophies have even helped my marriage!"

I can't be out there with you on calls, but I can help you by giving you a safe environment in which to practice before you are alone in the field. Consider these exercises a dry run for real-life selling and real-life rewards.

CHAPTER 1

Why Do You Want to Improve Your Closing Skills?

"The key to motivation is motive. It's the why. It's the deeper 'yes!' burning inside that makes it easier to say no to the less important."

- Stephen Covey

Why Do You Want to Improve Your Closing Skills?

Are you ready to write the next chapter in your career and life? Are you prepared to have your best year ever in sales? You've invested in this book for that purpose. Let's make the most of it. Right now. If you are prepared to go full out – to give it 100% – then you will gain tremendous value from this book – and it will be a lot of fun!

Motivation requires motive.

So, before we invest time in learning the skills of closing we must first tap into the deep well that is true motivation. Only then will it become sustained.

In management parlance we often talk about skill and will. Of course, skill is the knowledge and ability to execute a technique (like The Perfect Close). And, will is the willingness – the desire and passion – to actually use the skill.

Of these two, will is the most important. Because, if the willingness to use learned skills is absent, then all the skill in the world is irrelevant. Knowledge without action is useless. Skill in the presence of inaction is waste.

For that reason, we are going to focus on will before we focus on skill.

What you are about to learn is how to keep yourself motivated – forever. That is my promise to you. If you learn and apply the principles in the next two chapters, you will not only rev-up your motivation to the highest level, you'll be able to keep yourself motivated forever.

You Are in the Top 2%

Darren Hardy, the CEO of *Success* magazine, tells a story of standing in front of a large magazine rack at a popular bookstore with his friend.

The list of magazines included riveting titles like *Fencepost, Parking Review, Poultry World, The Hat Magazine, Potato Review, Wind Tunnel International,* and, my personal favorite, *Donkey Talk*.

While gazing at the tremendous number of magazines, he marveled out loud, "Man, I have something that everyone wants – SUCCESS! It's got big bold letters across the front of the magazine, and yet we're probably the worst-selling magazine up there because less than 2% of society is willing to invest in their own success."

And that's the reason I share this story with you. YOU are in that 2%. You are part of that special minority willing to invest in your own success. For that reason, I have the utmost respect for you. And, because you are willing to invest in yourself, you will be successful.

Darren Hardy, CEO, Success Magazine

I know better than anyone the sacrifices we make in sales. In sales, time is our only asset. We convert our time into money. For that reason, I have endeavored to make this a great experience for you; make this a great use of your time. For you, I want to be the resource I couldn't find when I was searching for all these answers.

So, indulge me if I make you just a little uncomfortable here and there, because I know what you are capable of.

The Three Lives of Salespeople

In more than 30 years of working with salespeople I've discovered that there are three kinds of salespeople.

1. Trapped
2. Comfortable
3. Energized

The Trapped Life

Trapped salespeople feel caged – trapped by their own habits and feelings. They feel uneasy, lack enthusiasm, don't have the time to accomplish what's needed and can't achieve financial freedom.

It's a crummy place.

Sometimes other people's expectations contribute to this. Sometimes it's our own expectations. Regardless of where it comes from, once you start feeling like this – as a salesperson – you're basically toast, because we telegraph these emotions to our prospects. And, transferring enthusiasm is an important part of selling.

The telltale sign of the Trapped Life is when the salesperson starts telling themselves, "No one understands me or my circumstances." It's not true, by the way. It's a lie and the ultimate cage.

If you're not feeling understood, ask yourself, "When was the last time I clearly articulated my goals and objectives to someone?" Then, do it – state them plainly and explicitly to someone. Then, both of you will know and understand where you're coming from.

If you ever find yourself thinking along these lines, the only way out is discipline and readiness. Don't avoid it. Instead, act toward it.

In the pages ahead, you will discover how to escape that cage. Now, let's move on.

The Comfortable Life

A lot of salespeople are living the Comfortable Life. You've achieved some success. You're satisfied, confident, and in control – and yet, if you admit it, you're a bit restless. It's a strange paradox. Even though you have plenty of reasons to say life is amazing, you still find yourself wondering if there's more. I know this feeling because I've been there.

The telltale sign of a salesperson in the Comfortable Life is "fine." That is, when someone asks you how you are doing, and you answer, "I'm fine." There's a certain tonality of voice to this response, if you know what I mean. And let me just tell you, if your significant other tells you they are "FINE" with that tonality – they are definitely NOT FINE.

So, when a salesperson tells me they are "fine," I know they are really searching for more – another quality, another level, another kind of life. It's the energized life.

The Energized Life

The Energized Life is a heightened level of energy and engagement. It's an enduring state of passion, satisfaction, and happiness. And, it's NOT triggered by COMFORT. It's triggered by – brace yourself – challenge.

Challenge itself creates energy. You know what I'm talking about. Think about a time when you were truly challenged (whether good or bad). Were you excited? Did you feel alive? Were you also just a little bit nervous? Maybe a lot bit nervous?

There's an anxious question of, "Can I really do this? I think I can do this!"

That little dose of uncertainty literally creates energy. And, that's what I want for you – the energized, charged-up life. So, I urge you to embrace the challenge – because it's the key to being and remaining fully energized.

Where Are You?

So, as we get started I want to ask you,

> "What life are you leading now?"
> "What level of energy are you bringing to your day, right now?"

A few years ago, I was chatting with a group of sales professionals. And, as sometimes happens, folks began to share their woes about what was happening in the market, in their company, and even at home.

Have you ever done that?

At first, I thought nothing of it. But, there were a few individuals that couldn't seem to get off the subject. One of them had been genuinely wronged. Another was facing a truly challenging situation. But here's the thing – by focusing so intently on their grievances they were letting this attitude seep into every aspect of their life – daily work, family time, and their general day-to-day happiness. They were so hung up on what was wrong, they were risking ruining everything.

Here's a news flash – everybody has had crap happen in their life. Crap at home, crap at work. My question is, "Did you ever bother to shower it off?"

I don't pretend it's easy. In fact, sometimes it's challenging. But, don't just sit back and complain about it. Instead, honor the challenge and stand up to it. Because when you overcome it, you'll have grown. You'll have reached the next level.

Life begins at the end of your comfort zone. Life will always be full of challenges. Growth from that challenge is optional. So, choose wisely. With the right attitude, you'll never fail. You'll win, or you'll learn.

What's Your Vision?

There's a book by Malcolm Gladwell that I highly recommend. It's called *Outliers*. The main conclusion of this book is that masters in any area – sports, music, business, or sales – simply practice more than others.

I want to challenge you to make a commitment to being world class at what you do. Never back down from the work. The best of the best don't have a magical advantage. They weren't born experts. They just practiced more.

They also have something else – vision. They have a motivating life vision of what they want.

Why do you get up in the morning? What are you trying to accomplish? What does success mean to you?

Maybe it's financial independence. Or doing something no one has ever done before. Or the happiness that comes from sharing with your family and others. Perhaps it's the feeling of control you get from having mastered something. Or the connected feeling you get by working for and with others as a team. Maybe you just want to give back somehow – to your family, your community, the world.

Whatever it is, it's important that you know. Because it literally drives everything else. I'll be straight-up with you. It's not an easy question for a lot of people. But the answers are absolutely KEY for sustained motivation.

What Are You Aiming At?

It is critical to know what you are aiming at because it provides clarity. Clarity about what you want eliminates the fog that comes with uncertainty. Without clarity your mind wastes 30-40% of its CPU cycles trying to figure out what you should do next. Reclaim that time by giving yourself clarity.

Before you start any focused activity, know exactly what you are aiming at. What is the outcome you are seeking? Before you start investing your precious energy climbing the ladder of success, make sure that it's leaning against the right wall.

So really ask yourself, "What is my vision? What do I really want right now?"

Here's why that is so important:

Your Job is an Excellent Vehicle

The job you have right now is an excellent vehicle to get you there – IF, you know what you want.

Unlike any other profession, sales offers unlimited possibilities. It scales. It can be the vehicle to accomplish your vision if you have clarity around what you want.

Need proof? Sales represents the 4th largest category of millionaires in the US. A full 5% of all millionaires are salespeople.

A small sampling of career sales professionals that have become millionaires:

Alfred Fuller - "Fuller Brush Man"	John H. Patterson - National Cash Register Co.
Ben Feldman - insurance	John Paul DeJoria - John Paul Mitchell Systems hair products
Bella Weems - Origami Owl	
Benjamin Franklin - printing	Larry Ellison - Oracle Corporation
B.R. Shetty - medical sales, NMC Healthcare	Mark Cuban - MicroSolutions et al
Brian Tracy - human development, real estate, imports, distribution	Mary Kay Ash - Mary Kay Cosmetics
	Napoleon Barragan - 1-800-Mattress
Dale Carnegie - author of *How to Win Friends and Influence People*	Napoleon Hill - author, reporter
	Nick Woodman - GoPro
David Ogilvy - Ogilvy & Mather	Ralph Lauren - fashion designer
Erica Feidner - Steinway & Sons pianos	Ron Popeil - Ronco
Francis G. "Buck" Rodgers - IBM	Ross Perot - IBM
Gary Vaynerchuk - retail wine, social media	Steve Jobs - Apple Inc.
Howard Schultz - Starbucks	Zig Ziglar - door-to-door, motivational speaking
Joe Girard - automotive sales	

There's also a second thing all these millionaire salespeople have in common...

The Power of Why

These millionaire salespeople know WHY they want what they want.

As I mentioned, motivation requires motive.

Once you've determined WHAT you want, ask yourself WHY you want it.

Some of you are probably rolling your eyes at this point. You might be thinking – for heaven's sake, James, I bought this workbook to improve my closing skills. Why are you going on and on about motivation?

I could have easily just given you The Perfect Close exercises and been done with it. But, I want to give you more than that. I want to give you something that will fire your motivation and make you excited to get up and at it each morning. I want to give you the sustained motivation that will allow you to not only apply the principles you are about to learn but to also be wildly successful. I want you to achieve your desired vision of the future.

And here's the truth – it's the answer to the WHY question that creates long-lasting, sustained motivation.

There's no getting around it. Willpower alone and the fear of consequences only work for a brief time. To attain long-lasting, sustained motivation we must tap into something much deeper and more meaningful. That's what answering the WHY question does. It connects our goal and, ultimately, our activities to the things we truly care about. And being connected to what we care about creates enduring motivation. Day in and day out. It's the energized life we talked about earlier.

So, indulge me for just a moment. Did you actually stop reading just a few paragraphs above to determine what you really want?

If you did, perhaps your answer was, "To make more money."

Then, you asked, "Why do I want more money?"

If you took the time to reflect on these questions, did it lead to even more questions? Like, what will having more money do for me? How will it make me feel? What emotional value is in it for me? These are the answers to the WHY question that will truly motivate you.

Once you answer the initial WHY question, you may need to drill down and go deeper with three or four follow-up questions to get to the core of your initial answer. And when you do, it will take you to a very cool place. With your newfound clarity you will be able to tap into a virtually limitless well of motivation.

I want everyone to experience this, so I've developed an exercise to help you.

EXERCISE #1 - Tapping Into Motivation - Part 1

Instructions: Individually, list the top 3 reasons you purchased this workbook.

(Why are you here doing this right now?)

Under Rating rate from 1-10 how motivating each of those reasons is to you.

Then, in the space below each reason write why you didn't rate each reason LOWER.

Reason		Rating
#1		
Why?		
#2		
Why?		
#3		
Why?		

Part 2

Instructions: Write your most motivating reason here: _____

Below, write what accomplishing that reason will enable you to do.
For each succeeding box, reference what the preceding box will enable you to do.

Because that will enable me to:	
And THAT will enable me to: ↓	
And THAT will enable me to: ↓	
And THAT will enable me to: ↓	
And THAT will enable me to: →	**Root Motivation**

What did you discover is your root motivation? Quite often, it is very personal and pure and noble. It gets to the very core of who you are, which I encourage you to share with others, because intent counts. We are motivated from the inside out.

Necessity – Another Level

Studies show that high performers are also motivated by necessity. They tap into the reasons that they must perform well in order to stay motivated. That necessity is a combination of internal standards (e.g. identity, beliefs, values, or expectations for excellence) and external demands (e.g. social obligations, competition, public commitments, deadlines).

What is your necessity? Why is it necessary that you succeed now? Who is counting on you? What identity, obsession, or duty requires that you succeed now?

BONUS: The Secret About WHY in Selling

People don't buy what you do as much as they buy why you do it. I recommend the book *Start with Why: How Great Leaders Inspire Everyone to Take Action* by Simon Sinek. Here's how it relates to sales.

EXERCISE #2 - The Secret About Why in Selling

Answer this: What do you do for a living?

Answer: _____

_____

Now circle the answer to these questions:		
Does anyone else do that same thing?	Yes	No
Could another company use my same answer for their company?	Yes	No
Did your answer focus on your actions, or the benefits that your actions bring your customer?	Actions	Benefits

Perhaps your answer was something like, "I sell practice management solutions to medical facilities." Or, simply, "I'm in sales."

Not very inspiring, is it?

To create an inspiring answer, we need to focus on the "why" rather than the "what".

Focusing on "what" we do fails to differentiate us from competitors. It isn't client-focused and it isn't motivating.

What if we swapped that answer out with something like: "I preserve the freedom of physicians to focus on caring for patients by facilitating and streamlining the business side of their practice."

Wow. With this answer, you go way beyond simply stating what you do by revealing what beneficial effects your activities create, which is essentially a WHY answer.

What type of response might you get from the person who's just asked this very basic question, a person who might just happen to be your next client? It might sound something like this:

- **Acquaintance:** "Interesting. How do you do it?"
- **Salesperson:** "By eliminating all the non-care-related obligations physicians have, so they can focus on just caring for their patients."
- **Acquaintance:** "That's great. What do you do to accomplish that?"
- **Salesperson:** "We do it with specially designed automation software and services that offload administration duties from a physician's workload, allowing them to focus exclusively on patient care."

Is this substitution more compelling?

The interesting thing is, with a compelling WHY people will naturally take us to the HOW and WHAT we do. It looks a little like this:

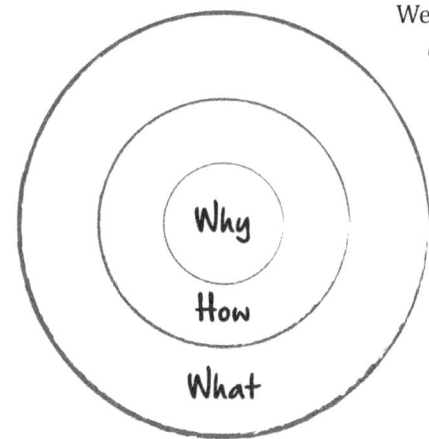

We are motivated from the inside out and that applies to not only ourselves but to everyone we encounter, especially our customers.

If you want sustained, long-lasting motivation to reach your goals, tie them to the objects and ideals that you really care about. The WHYs in your life give your goals meaning – and enduring motivation to stick to your plan. Your WHY-power becomes your WILL-power. Once you know your WHY, the execution part will come easily.

Your brain's natural progression looks like this:

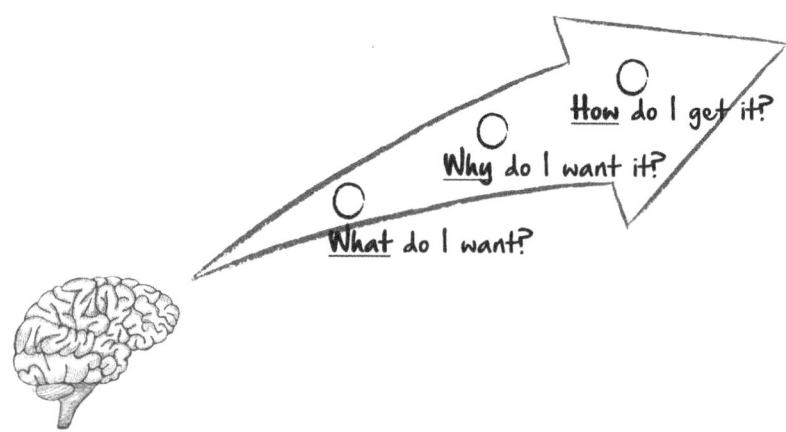

With the WHAT and the WHY in place, your brain will automatically ask the next question which is, HOW, "How do I get it?" Your brain will naturally start creating ideas, energy, and motivation to that end, and you'll be tapping into a drive that will last you a lifetime.

CHAPTER 2

Sales is Service

Fifty to 90% of all sales encounters end without any commitment being asked for whatsoever. Why do you suppose that is?

In the end, it boils down to two reasons: Will and Skill.

That is, the salesperson either doesn't have the *skill* to ask for a commitment or they don't have the *will* to ask for a commitment.

The good news is that you have in your hands, right now, the best practice in asking for commitments and closing sales. It's just two questions, zero pressure and 95% effective. So, if you have ever been challenged by not having the skill, your answer is right here.

The bad news is, it is far more common that will is the root cause of reluctance. Let's address that right now.

There are two primary reasons why will is often a challenge for sales professionals and both are a matter of perception.

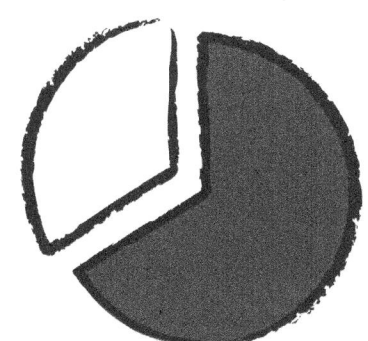

50%-90% of sales encounters end with no commitment being asked for

Why Sales Has a Bad Reputation

Sales is a much-maligned career. Ask the average member of society what they think of when they hear the word "salesperson" and you'll get four negative sentiments to every one positive sentiment. Words that often come up include pushy, sleazy, slimy, cheesy, etc. – they almost sound like the lost seven dwarfs of sales!

There is a 4 to 1 negative sentiment regarding sales.

Why is there so much negative sentiment regarding sales professionals?

The reason is that for many years there was an asymmetry of information between the seller and the buyer. That is, in the past, sellers held all the cards. And this asymmetry of information allowed unscrupulous salespeople to take advantage of buyers – which they sometimes did.

These self-serving and unethical salespeople of the past created the current perception the world has about the sales profession, which can be captured nicely in the phrase "buyer beware."

The Modern Era of Sales

Things have changed dramatically in recent times. Today, there is very little asymmetry of information between the seller and the buyer, and the balance of power has shifted to the buyer. Today, it is not uncommon for the buyer to have even more information than the seller.

Consider your last car purchase for example. Did you search online and conduct some research before going to a dealership? How much information were you able to find? Today, you can find nearly everything you need to know about a given product or service online, can't you? This is one of the biggest reasons the game has changed.

The conditions that formed the historical reputation of sales no longer exist and haven't existed for some time. And with very few exceptions, salespeople do not manipulate or use asymmetry of information to take advantage of buyers anymore. We just don't sell that way. We don't sell that way because ethics matter. And because the long-term repercussions of selling that way are negative and short-sighted. Genuinely creating win-win relationships with clients is the only way to achieve sustainable success.

And yet, that old perception lingers on, doesn't it?

Negative Association

So, a big part of the "will" problem is that honest, ethical people don't want to be identified with the negative associations of yesteryear's sales world, despite the fact that it no longer exists. Their honesty and ethics affect their willingness to ask for commitments. Can you relate to this?

Fear of Rejection

There is also this notion that sales professionals fear rejection. They fear getting the "no" answer, and that causes them to hesitate when asking for commitments. This has been studied extensively, and we will touch more on this topic ahead. The truth is, salespeople aren't so much afraid of getting rejected so much as they are afraid of damaging the relationship. And, as it turns out, 99% of the closing methods being taught are manipulative and have been proven to damage the relationship. Even without this proof, sales professionals can sense this. So, rather than risk the relationship by using a manipulative tactic – they choose to do nothing.

This is the number one challenge to closing sales.

The Solution

The solution to these challenges is twofold:
1. Learn a method of asking for commitments that enhances the relationship rather than damaging it.
2. Discover that selling is serving, and that by embracing this fact we can shed all the negative associations of sales.

Selling is Serving

I have spent the majority of my selling career in the healthcare space. In healthcare, sales often takes on a very different feel than in other industries. Let me illustrate with a story.

Kaiba Gionfriddo

Kaiba Gionfriddo is the son of Bryan and April Gionfriddo in Akron, Ohio. Kaiba was born with a defective trachea that caused him to stop breathing almost every day after he reached six weeks old. Each time he stopped breathing, April and Bryan would furiously pump his chest to get air into their son's lungs. They performed CPR on him almost every day and ordinary doctors did not expect him to live.

Imagine what that would be like as a parent – knowing that at any moment your child might stop breathing and die – and for Kaiba, helplessly struggling for air. It's a tragic situation.

Enter Hope

Eventually Kaiba and his parents found Dr. Glenn Green at the University of Michigan's C.S. Mott Children's Hospital. Dr. Green had developed an amazing 3D-printed medical splint that could be applied to Kaiba's trachea and save his life. Made from a special biodegradable material the splint looks like just a little piece of plastic.

This biodegradable 3D-printed medical splint was a new technology. So, Dr. Green had to use an emergency provision to get FDA approval to use this tracheal splint to try and save Kaiba's life. It was a challenge, but the FDA gave approval, and the procedure was scheduled.

The Miracle of Life

The procedure was a success. The biodegradable, 3D-printed medical splint saved Kaiba's life. Before this procedure, babies with severe tracheobronchomalacia had little chance of surviving. Today, Kaiba is an active, healthy, six-year-old in elementary school with a bright future.

An Emotional Story

This is an emotional story. We all marvel with gratitude at the efforts that saved this young child's life. We can sense and connect with the goodness of it. We're all grateful to call ourselves part of humanity when we see efforts such as this. And we say to ourselves, "If I could save a life that way, I would do it." Don't we?

The Big Surprise

Did you know there was a lot of selling going on here?

Dr. Green had to sell Bryan and April on the efficacy of his device. Dr. Green also had to sell the FDA on his emergency appeal to approve the device. The CT & MRI scans that made the printing possible were purchased from a manufacturer. The lasers and 3D printers and biodegradable materials required to print the device also came about through a sales transaction. The person responsible for making this sale is Scott Hollister.

We don't hear too much about the selling part of these stories, do we? And yet, there are thousands of stories just like this one with an honest and ethical salesperson who contributed to yet another happy ending.

The Big Question

Let me ask you a question. Do you think anyone, including yourself, who reads this story would associate negatively with the efforts of Scott Hollister? Of course not. Why? Because he was contributing to saving people's lives. It doesn't *feel* like selling when we put that way. So, why should anyone see this type of sale differently than any other kind of sale?

When we can see the positive effects that sales solutions have on people's lives, we can make the connection between selling and serving. Without sales to fund efforts, this splint would never have been made – and a child's life would have been lost.

These dramatic examples help us see what selling truly is – service.

Selling is an act of service.

Selling Is Noble

Not every solution aims to deliver lofty goals such as saving lives, feeding the hungry, or easing people's pain with medications. Yet they all endeavor to serve and improve. Some solutions allow people to communicate or travel over great distances. Other solutions simplify everyday tasks allowing people to focus on higher-value activities – like work or family. And, there are thousands more.

Each solution that we sell helps someone achieve a goal, fulfill a dream, or avert a crisis. Each solution, regardless of how large or how small, helps a real person move from where they are, to where they want to be.

Selling is an Act of Service

Helping a customer move towards their goal is an act of service. It shouldn't be difficult or stressful at all. It should be easy. Easy in the same way we say to ourselves, "If I could save a life that way, I would do it, without hesitation."

Because selling is serving.

The Curse of Distraction

Sometimes we lose sight of that fact. Sometimes we get so caught up in our own selfish motives (what's in it for us) or administrative details that we forget we're working to help our clients achieve their goals.

But it doesn't have to be that way...

Conclusion

Selling *is* hard sometimes. But it is 100% noble and 100% satisfying, if you make it that way.

Remember that selling is an act of service, and in so doing, we enrich both our lives and our customer's lives in a virtuous cycle. There should be no hesitation in that belief. When we keep service in mind, selling becomes motivating in its own right.

CHAPTER 3

Mindset

 **EXERCISE #3** - **Why Do You Want to Close Sales?**

Instructions: List one opportunity that you are pursuing.

Now, think about your driving desire to move this opportunity forward.

- Why do I want to advance this sale?
- Why do I want to close?
- What is my motivation?

In the form below, write your Reasons to those questions (most people have less than five). Review your list. Which is your top driver? Which is secondary and so on? Prioritize them in the Priority column.

Opportunity _____

Reasons	Priority
#1	
#2	
#3	
#4	
#5	

The initial results from this exercise usually produce answers like, "I want to get paid." Or, "I want something that money can buy." And while these may be good motivations, in most cases, they are not things that we would communicate directly to a prospective customer.

What you might find extremely alarming, however, is you are already communicating these desires unintentionally. And these messages can have a very big effect on your results. Going into a client interaction with the wrong mindset can negatively affect your outcome.

Conversely, the right mindset will positively affect your outcome. And that is the object of this chapter – to help you adopt the mindset that will positively affect all your interactions.

How We Communicate Our Intentions Unintentionally

There are three main ways we communicate our intentions unintentionally:

1. Mirror Neurons
2. Micro-expressions
3. Paralanguage

Neurophysiologist
Dr. Giacomo Rizzolatti

Mirror Neurons

In the 1990s an Italian neurophysiologist named Giacomo Rizzolatti made an amazing discovery. He and his team were researching brain function using monkeys as test subjects. The monkeys were being monitored by machines that registered their brain activity. The scientists would encourage the monkeys to do various activities by offering a reward – a peanut, a food they love. When a monkey receives and eats a peanut the pleasure centers of their brains light up like a Christmas tree.

One day, one of the researchers ate a peanut in front of one of the monkeys, and an amazing thing happened. The monkey's pleasure centers lit up, just as if the monkey had eaten the peanut himself. This was an unexpected development, and after much more investigation Rizzolatti's research team discovered that both monkeys and humans have something called mirror neurons that mimic both the actions and emotions of those around them (simian or human).

Much research into mirror neurons has been completed since that time, and through the miracle of Functional Magnetic Resonance Imaging (fMRI) modern science can now watch the brain's responses to stimuli in real time. We now know that mirror neurons are involved in a tremendous number of psycho-social areas including language, learning, self-awareness, and most importantly for sales – understanding intentions and empathy.

A key takeaway here is that we are an empathic species. When we see another living being experience an emotion such as happiness or sorrow, our mirror neurons cause us to experience that same emotion along with them. There is a whole invisible level of communication going on.

Thus, mirror neurons make it possible to understand another person's point of view, and just as importantly as we'll see in a moment, their intent. It is important for us to be aware of these distinctions so that we understand the involuntary messages our prospective clients are receiving from us.

Micro-expressions

You may be familiar with the TV series *Lie to Me* which aired from 2009–2011. It was inspired by the work of renowned psychologist Paul Ekman who served as a consultant to the show. In the series Dr. Cal Lightman and his team used their knowledge of body language and facial expressions to effectively act as human polygraph machines and uncover the truth for law enforcement, law firms, corporations, and individuals. The results are both entertaining and educational. For example, in the pilot episode Lightman interviews a man who refuses to speak at all, yet Lightman still could discern vital information by gauging the man's reactions to verbal cues.

Ekman began his research into nonverbal communication in the mid-1950s and focused on developing techniques for measuring nonverbal communication. Through empirical research of the muscular movements that create facial expression, he discovered that human beings are capable of more than 10,000 facial expressions – 3,000 of which are relevant to emotion.

Psychologist Dr. Paul Ekman

Thanks to Ekman, we understand micro-expressions as brief, involuntary human facial expressions derived from immediate, inner emotions. Micro-expressions occur most frequently in high-stakes situations where people have something to lose or gain. Micro-expressions also occur when a person is consciously trying to conceal signs of how they are feeling, or when they do not consciously know how they are feeling. Unlike regular facial expressions, micro-expressions are very brief, lasting only $\frac{1}{25}$th to $\frac{1}{15}$th of a second and virtually impossible to hide.

These systems are constantly in play. Your body is continuously sending signals that reveal your intentions and emotions. And just as importantly, your subconscious and autonomic systems are working 24/7 reading the body language of others to decode their intentions and emotions.

It is a deciphering system to determine friend or foe, honesty or deception – to decide if you are on their side or not. Basic, simple detections like these might be described as intuition or a gut reaction, but what is critical to understand is that our intentions are very important when interacting with others.

Paralanguage

You also give out similar signals with your voice. This, too, is mostly an unconscious activity. It's called paralanguage and is the part of verbal communication that changes meaning via volume, pitch, intonation, and prosody. Paralinguistic speech plays a very important role in human interactions because every spoken communication contains these non-lexical speech signals.

Unlike micro-expressions, individuals have greater control over paralanguage. In most cases attitudes are expressed intentionally while emotions are more often expressed unintentionally. Thus, paralanguage, while important, is secondary to visual cues. Nevertheless, it is important to be aware of the non-lexical messages we may be sending via our volume, pitch, speed, and intonation.

Conscious Control?

Your prospective clients are consciously and unconsciously detecting your involuntary signals which ultimately develops their general impressions about you. Upon learning these facts, the typical reaction I hear from salespeople is something like, "How can I possibly control all of these things in my interactions with clients?"

Consciously, you can't. Evidence indicates all but the most unusual subjects (patients with special mental conditions, for example) are unable to affect the myriad involuntary signals we continually transmit.

Further, the ability to detect intention develops at a very early age – emerging in children as young as 18 months and sometimes even earlier. So, basically, we're all experts at reading other people's intentions.

The good news, and the point of this chapter, is that you don't have to worry about your micro-expressions or attempt to control them, if you adopt the right mindset. With the right intentions these signals will automatically be working for you without you having to think about it. Your body will be sending all the right messages naturally.

With the right mindset your body will:
- Form the right, positive micro-expressions
- Deliver the ideal tonality
- Express the emotions with which you want your prospective client to empathize
- Communicate the right intention to maximize trust and rapport

All of this will greatly improve both the experience and the outcomes of your interactions with others.

What Is the Right Mindset?

To know what the ideal mindset is, it's important to understand what happens from a psychological perspective in the initial seconds of any interaction. Among the first is a determination of the intent of the person we're encountering. Are they friend or foe? Immediately following that, the brain ascertains whether the other person has the actual ability to enact those intentions. These two things form much of the basis for determining trust and competency.

To determine the attributes that have the greatest impact on interpersonal communication, scientists have conducted a tremendous number of studies. And, by all accounts with more than 200 attributes having been tested, the most important and dominate attributes can be placed into two categories: warmth and competence.

While both warmth and competence consistently rise to the top of attributes in all studies, evidence shows that warmth judgments are primary. That is, warmth is judged before competence, and warmth carries greater weight in affecting social reactions.

People infer warmth from the perceived motives and intentions of another person, and those perceptions are gleaned not only from voluntary actions but also from involuntary messages the other person conveys.

So, for our intentions to be perceived as warm, it's vital that we emanate the related traits that science has identified from the warmth attribute. These include:
- pure intent
- friendliness
- helpfulness
- sincerity
- trustworthiness
- and morality (doing the right thing)

These are the signals we want our body to be sending.

EXERCISE #4 – The Message of Your Motives - Part 1

Instructions: Complete the following phrase by inserting each of your motivations listed in Exercise #3:

Sentence Stem	Reason/Motivation	Signal
Thanks for meeting with me today my top priority is to…		
Thanks for meeting with me today my top priority is to…		
Thanks for meeting with me today my top priority is to…		
Thanks for meeting with me today my top priority is to…		
Thanks for meeting with me today my top priority is to…		

Are these statements you would be willing to say to a prospective client? Would any of them be appropriate to say to clients?

Part 2

Instructions: Now, under the Signal column, categorize each Reason/Motivation as:

- Self-Focused
- Client-Focused
- Mutually Beneficial

Group Discussion: Are these the signals you want to be sending. If not, what would need to change to send the ideal signals listed above?

Commission Breath

Most people who complete the exercise reveal motivators and drivers like, "I want to get paid," or "I want something money can buy." When your prospect senses that your intention is "all about you" they become more guarded.

As a sales manager I've received both good and bad feedback regarding salespeople. One client said they could tell the salesperson was only in it for himself, and they refused to do business with him. To describe their interaction with this salesperson, the client coined a term that has stuck in my mind forever; he called it "commission breath." It fits so perfectly.

That is exactly the type of impression we are trying to avoid. Prospective buyers experience a great deal of concern and trepidation during the decision-making process – especially when the product is beyond their own area of expertise since their ignorance creates risk. They are concerned that an unscrupulous salesperson could take advantage of them – that they'll be sold the wrong product or, at the very least, they won't get the best value. And when a client decides that a salesperson's intentions are not aligned with their best interests, in most cases, the deal is off.

Often, even when our intentions are good, the larger the opportunity is, the harder it is not to think about what's in it for us. It is ironic, then, that despite our intent to earn money in an ethical way, when we enter an interaction with our minds focused on what we hope to get, our autonomic system sends precisely the wrong signal for the best outcome.

In Sales Intent Is Weighed More Heavily Than Competence

There are two determinations that buyers make each time they meet with us.

1. What is this person's intent (good or bad)?
2. Can this person execute that intention?

When purchasing something outside our expertise, because of our ignorance, the sales agent has the upper hand and the ability to possibly take advantage of us. Inexperience leaves us vulnerable. Therefore, we must rely primarily on the first discriminator – intent.

Because intent is so heavily weighted in sales situations we must transmit the right intentions. The key is to adopt a mindset that will have us transmitting the right intentions – one where we genuinely want to help the other person in a friendly and ethical way.

There is no need to change your personality or become something you are not. By genuinely trying to help the other person in a friendly and ethical way, our autonomic system will take over and automatically transmit all the right messages.

How to Adopt the Right Mindset

Why are we going on and on about mindset and good intentions when you purchased a book about closing?

Because intent matters more than technique.

Intent > Technique

You can learn the most effective techniques, but if you enter your opportunity with "commission breath," it won't matter. Conversely, when a client can detect your genuine intention to help, you can butcher the technique, say gobbledygook, and it will still work out because intent matters more than technique.

The question now becomes, "How do I get myself into the right mindset?"

There are three simple steps you can take before any interaction to adopt the right mindset:

1. Lose the ego.
2. Create positive emotion.
3. Enter with the right intent.

1. Lose the Ego

Ego is about you and self-importance – either what you hope to receive or the desire to impress others. A strong sense of self-esteem is good and important to the concept of competency. However, because warmth and intention are weighted more heavily in sales situations, we want to maximize our warmth factor and transmit that we have the client's best interests at heart.

EXERCISE #5 - Lose the Ego - Part 1

Instruction: When you hear that someone has an "ego" or that they are an "egomaniac" what thoughts and words come to mind? Write them below.

Associations With The Word "Ego"		

- Part 2

Are these the kind of individuals that you enjoy working with?

Now consider the types of individuals you do enjoy working with. What are their qualities and attributes? Write those in the space below.

Qualities & Attributes of Individuals That Are Enjoyable to Work With		

 Group Discussion: As a group, share and compare the qualities and attributes of individuals you enjoy working with. Write these words on a white board or flip chart.

How might you incorporate these qualities and attributes into your interactions with clients?

Enter into your initial interactions with customers by emulating the qualities and attributes that make you enjoyable to work with. Enter without any ego-based agenda. Lose the ego. Remain confident and competent but enter your initial interaction *tabula rasa* (with a blank slate) and no defined agenda, other than how you can best help the prospective client.

Ego-driven desires cause your body to send the wrong signals.

2. Create Positive Emotion

Consider using these recall and posture techniques to create the ideal emotional state before your meetings.

Positive Recall

By vividly remembering an experience when we were emanating the right attributes, we put ourselves into the same state. By recalling these memories prior to a sales encounter, we cause our bodies to send the right signals.

> Example of a positive memory I often use to get me in the right state before meeting with clients.
>
> One day, out of the blue, I received a call from a long-time friend. He shared that his company had a new product they were trying to market.
>
> My friend was not in sales, and he asked me to visit their office and coach them on how they might improve sales. He wasn't hiring me as a consultant; he was simply asking for a favor. I could tell he was calling because they were in trouble. Naturally, I agreed to help.
>
> Despite this being described as a "casual chat" with his company's top executives, I understood that by bringing me in, he was putting his reputation on the line. So, it was important to me that this meeting reflect well on my friend. I invested some time learning all about their product, their processes, the new market they were in, and their results thus far. Out of respect for my friend I wanted the meeting to be as helpful as possible.
>
> At the beginning of the meeting I described what I believed I had uncovered about their situation and asked if I was on target. I wasn't. About 20% of the information I had gathered was incorrect. After these top executives corrected the information and filled in the gaps, we began a productive conversation about what I had seen work elsewhere and different ways we could approach their situation.
>
> It was an ultra-productive session where I was freely sharing my experience, and they were receiving new and helpful information. They were so engaged that they bumped their next meeting to continue the conversation. We concluded with an excellent vibe, and they thanked me profusely. As their CEO walked me to the parking lot he asked what he owed me for the visit. I explained that I was doing it out of friendship for my buddy.
>
> Weeks later, my friend shared that they had experienced great success with some of the ideas we discussed. Then unexpectedly I received a check in the mail from the CEO along with a thank-you note. It was quite a surprise. I recall feeling satisfied and validated that I had truly been helpful that day.

Once you are able to re-experience the emotion of your memory, your autonomic system will take care of the rest. Ideally, spend about two minutes doing this to let the physiological processes take effect, and your body will begin telegraphing that you are genuinely trying to help in a friendly and ethical way.

EXERCISE #6 - Positive Recall – Your Own Positive Memories

In this exercise you will be putting a positive memory of yours to paper and making it as vivid as possible.

Instructions:

Step 1. – Individually, recall a time when you felt helpful and friendly. Ideally, choose an experience where you emanated the following attributes: pure intent, friendliness, helpfulness, sincerity, trustworthiness and morality (doing the right thing).

Step 2. – Describe the event in the space below. Make it as vivid as possible. What did it look, sound, smell, feel and taste like? Try to relive the experience as you write.

Step 3. – In the area labeled "Positive Attributes" write out all the positive attributes you can associate with your memory.

Step 4. – As a group, share your memory with someone. How did you feel during the experience and how did you feel just now while remembering and writing it out?

Note: Repeat this exercise as many times as needed so you have an inventory of memories to positively affect your mental and emotional state.

My Positive Memory

Positive Attributes

Posture

The posture technique derives from relatively new findings made by Amy Cuddy and Dana Carney who discovered that postural expressions not only affect people's emotions, but amazingly, they also affect hormone levels. Cuddy and Carney found that by faking body postures associated with a desired emotion, people can positively improve their hormone response. Assuming power poses, for example, increases testosterone, decreases cortisol, increases an appetite for risk, and causes people to perform better in job interviews.

For our purpose we want to adopt a posture of friendliness, helpfulness, sincerity, and trustworthiness.

EXERCISE #7 - Posture to Improve Emotion and Physiology

To invoke these emotional qualities (and ideal hormonal and physiological responses), the posture we want to adopt is known as the "Welcome Gesture" or "Mock Hug".

Instructions: Stand up and adopt the following posture to practice the technique:

Arms are open, rounded and relaxed about waist height. Palms are tilted about 45 degrees upwards. Shoulders are relaxed and down (not up near the neck). Legs are not crossed and may even be widened a bit past shoulder width, if that is comfortable. Smile warmly—the smile is a big part. Consider the whole posture as a mock hug or welcoming gesture.

Casually and with flowing variation, maintain this posture for two minutes or so. According to research, it takes two minutes for the hormone response to kick in.

Many people find it easier to get into it completely if they also say something to themselves like:

- "There you are!"
- "I love you guys!"
- "It's so great to see you!"
- "Here I am! I'm here to help!"

Both Positive Recall and the Posture Technique are intended to be done before you meet with your client and only take about two minutes. With a little practice you can do both simultaneously.

BONUS – Make Yourself Feel Awesome!

As a bonus, experiment with making yourself feel awesome using the same technique. With these two poses.

Wonder Woman – Stand with your feet apart, your hands on your hips, and your chin tilted upward. Hold for two minutes.

The Champion – Stand with your feet widely apart and stretch your hands overhead in a "V" shape (think "V" for victory). Hold for two minutes.

Notice the difference in your confidence and mood elevation.

3. Enter with the Right Intent

Positive self-talk improves performance in decision making, strategy formulation, academics, sports, overcoming dysfunctions and bad habits, and other complex skills.

To program ourselves to transmit the right intent, we're going to use a couple of affirmations that will quickly prime our bodies to send the right messages about our intent.

Being genuine, say something like the following before each interaction:
- "You know, I genuinely care about this client. I'm excited to see what they have going on."
- "I'm sure I can help these guys. I can't wait to see what I can do for this client."
- "I want to make a big difference for these guys."
- "I'm curious to learn how I can best help these people. I'm thrilled to find out what I can do for them."

These statements (when said genuinely) will cause you to project the right intentions to others.

Exercise #8 - Affirmations

Instructions: Using what you've learned and the examples above craft one or more of your own affirmations to prime yourself before each meeting:

Affirmation: _____

Affirmation: _____

Affirmation: _____

Share your affirmation with the group along with why you chose that particular affirmation.

Affirmation Triggers

Mental triggers are environmental conditions that trigger thoughts and feelings. Develop mental triggers to operationalize your affirmations and permanently install them into your life. Here are just a few examples:

- **Calendar Trigger** – As I review my calendar of appointments I say to myself, "I can do a lot of good here. I can't wait to see what I can do for these clients."

- **Doorway Trigger** – Each time I walk through a doorway I say to myself, "I will find the good in this room. I am going to serve everyone in here."

- **Getting Out of The Car Trigger** – Before I step out of the car at a client site I say to myself, "I'm sure we can help these guys. Let's go make a big difference for them."

- **Phone Trigger** – Before making each call I say to myself, "Everyone loves happy people. I will bring happiness and helpfulness to this call."

There is unlimited potential when it comes to developing your own mental triggers. You will find them useful in both your professional and personal life.

Using what you've learned and the examples above develop your own mental set of mental triggers.

Environmental Trigger	Affirmation

Group Discussion: After creating your triggers, gather into groups of 3 or 4 and share your mental triggers. What new ideas did you get by hearing the triggers and affirmations of others?

The next time you're on a call with an associate, try saying one or more of the triggers out loud and see if it has any effect on their attitude.

Share Your Intent

All the exercises to this point are intended to be done immediately before meeting with your client and can be completed in less than three to five minutes. This prepares you to transmit the right signals in the first seconds of your interaction, which is important because that's when judgments regarding your warmth and intention happen.

There is something else you can do while in the presence of your client to project the right intention – actually say it. Tell the client what your intentions are. Clients look for congruence between your verbalization and your body language, and when they match, you will improve your impression by yet another level.

There are many ways to share your intent with clients, and you will need to adjust your message depending on the context of each meeting. With that in mind, here are some examples to help you create your own intention statements.

- **Short & Sweet** – Early in my career I was in a technical resource role and was always paired up with another salesperson. After introducing myself, I'd simply add, "My job is to make sure you get what you want." That always resonated with clients and accurately conveyed that I was their advocate.
- **Premature Questions on Differentiators** – Very often prospects will jump the gun and ask for pricing or competitive differentiators before any of the preliminaries are complete. "Why should we purchase you over your competition?" they might ask prematurely. A possible response is, "Well I think we might be a good match, but I'm not 100% confident yet. My goal is to get you a solution that exactly matches what you want. Share with me a little about…" In this way, I convey that I suspect potential exists, but as their advocate I would like to know more about them and what they are trying to accomplish.
- **Premature Questions on Price** – With the early pricing question I often use, "My whole career, my formula for success has simply been to do a great job for clients, and then those clients in return have helped me get new business. That means it's not important that I get maximum profit from a deal. I just need to make sure I am in the black. So, I promise I'll get you the best deal possible once we know there is a great fit." Sometimes I'll then redirect to discovery with, "So with that in mind can you share with me…?" This dialogue accomplishes many things, but what I want to accentuate here is that I've conveyed that my intent is to get them the best deal possible, and that lets us move on to the important details without getting embroiled into a conversation about price.
- **Introduction** – Another way you can convey your intent is to weave it into your introduction about your company and culture. An example might be, "What I've come to learn after X years in the business is that every client is unique. So, our goal is to get you a solution that is exactly what you want. Most of the time we can do that – but not always – and by working together, we can identify all the dimensions of what you're looking for, and make sure we have a solution that exactly meets your needs." In this way we are conveying our intention that we want what they want, and that will allow us to smoothly move through the process of understanding each other.

These examples should get your juices flowing so you can create your own intention statements that will be congruent with the messages your autonomic system is sending. Together they strongly communicate your intentions to genuinely help the other person in a friendly and ethical way.

 **EXERCISE #9** - Intention Statements

Instructions: Using what you've learned and the examples above create your own intention statement for the following circumstances:

Situation	Intention Statement
Short & Sweet Introduction	
Full Introduction	
Premature Questions on Differentiators	

 Group Discussion: After creating your intention statements gather together into groups of 3 or 4 and share your intention statements. What new ideas did you get by hearing the intention statements of others?

For solo reader: After creating your intention statements share them with your manager or another seller. What new ideas did you get by hearing their feedback?

 CLOSING SECRET - Intent matters more than technique.

Conclusion

Having the right mindset will improve your experience, your prospective client's experience, and improve your outcomes in a most positive way.

The techniques and exercises outlined in this chapter will get your mindset in the right place and get your body transmitting the right messages, in as little as three to five minutes.

After you have practiced it consistently for some time, you will discover that you are simply always in the mindset. It will become a permanent part of you, and you will automatically transmit this signal 24/7. This is an amazing state to be in from a happiness and personal achievement perspective and may be worth as much as the rest of the techniques you are about to learn. It also hints at a deeper meaning of what selling is – service with pure intent. I encourage you to adopt it not just in selling but also in your everyday life.

CHAPTER 4

What Is Closing?

 **EXERCISE #10** - What is Closing?

Instructions: Write out your answer(s) to the question below.

If in a group, use a flip chart or white board

"What is Closing?"

 Group Discussion: Discuss the different perspectives given. How practical are the answers? What is implied? Is there a best definition?

What exactly is closing? There are many definitions. Some are quite good, others less so. For example, "Doing whatever you have to do to get the customer to sign," isn't so good in my book.

"Asking for the sale," "Asking for the order," and similar definitions are common. These essentially boil down to, "That thing you say that gets the customer to buy." While useful for some purposes, this definition perpetuates one of the biggest problems with closing techniques – that it paints the close as an all or nothing request. And as we shall see, most sales cannot be treated this way.

Other definitions are more broad and holistic. Like, "Closing is everything you do from the beginning of the sale to final completion of the transaction and beyond." I believe this, by the way. The problem is that these definitions essentially redefine closing as all of selling, which makes the definition so broad that it limits its usefulness. And we're only defining this term so we can get better results, right?

For our purposes we are going to accept Neil Rackham's definition of a close and build on it. Here is Rackham's definition: "A close is anything that puts the customer in a position involving some kind of commitment."

> *"A close is anything that puts the customer in a position involving some kind of commitment."*
> *— Neil Rackham*

This gives us a workable definition that fits somewhere between, "It's all or nothing" and, "It's everything." This is an important aspect of The Perfect Close because while we sometimes get a final completed transaction, many times what we achieve is really an advance. For the most part, I'll use the terms *close* and *advance* synonymously. That will allow us to discuss the idea of "closing on a minor-step," "going for a minor-close," "advancing the sale," or "getting an advance." All of these essentially mean the same thing.

Neil Rackham & The Definitions of Closing

The selling world owes a debt of gratitude to Neil Rackham who in the 1980s conducted the largest sales study ever and authored a book called *SPIN Selling*.

In *SPIN Selling*, Rackham created some very valuable definitions.

Closing – Anything that puts the customer in a position involving some kind of commitment.

He also coined two new selling terms you should be familiar with. The first is Advance and the second is Continuation.

Advance – Progressing the sale forward in a little way.

Continuation – A situation where the sale will continue, yet no specific action has been agreed upon by the customer to move forward.

We will be building on these and more of Rackham's work as we progress.

Neil Rackham

EXERCISE #11 – Facts & Myths of Closing

Instructions: Reflect on each statement below and circle the level to which you agree.

After scoring all seven statements total your numbers and enter the result at the bottom of the first column.

	Strongly Disagree	Disagree	Neutral	Agree	Strongly Agree
Closing techniques (in general) are effective ways to close the sale.	1	2	3	4	5
More frequent closing attempts are better. More attempts increase the odds of closing.	1	2	3	4	5
All sales are the same. The principles and closing techniques that work for small opportunities also apply to large opportunities.	1	2	3	4	5
Use of closing techniques is a positive way to show that you want the customer's business.	1	2	3	4	5
Customers are happier after making a decision so pushing them to make a decision is for their own good.	1	2	3	4	5
Closing attempts are unnecessary. Customers will close you when they are ready.	1	2	3	4	5
Salespeople fear asking for commitment because they fear rejection.	1	2	3	4	5
Total Score: < ---- **Total Row**					

Score Key

28-35	Learning Opportunity	Scientific data does not support these statements.
15-17	Mixed	You are clear on a few issues but may have fallen victim to some of the myths of closing.
7-14	Excellent	Scientific data supports your view that these statements are incorrect.

Group Discussion: Discuss your score and your perspectives on each statement. How do others perceive each statement?

Facts & Myths About Closing

There are many misconceptions about selling and any one of them can seriously undermine your selling efforts. You are about to learn the statistical truths about closing, and knowing these will help your sales in a very big way.

Myth #1 – Closing Gambits Work

Some people call them "techniques," but I call them "gambits" because they are typically manipulative. The premise behind all of these closes is that they actually work.

People who have a lot of faith in closing gambits will be surprised to learn that Rackham tested the correlation between sales success and a salesperson's attitude toward closing techniques, and he discovered that salespeople with a favorable attitude towards closing techniques actually performed 21% worse than those with an unfavorable attitude.

He went on to test the success of closing techniques (gambits) after training and discovered that the use of closing techniques/gambits reduced sales by approximately 15%.

FACT: Closing gambits are negatively related to success and actually decrease sales success by about 15%.

Myth #2 – Always Be Closing

Thanks to Alec Baldwin in the movie *Glengarry Glen Ross* we all know the ABCs of sales: Always Be Closing. We also sometimes hear this as the axiom, "Close early and often." Unfortunately, this has been tested, and beyond the first attempt there is a negative correlation between closing frequency and sales-call success.

In his first study on the topic, Rackham found that high-close calls (calls that averaged 5.8 closing behaviors) had a success rate of approximately 37%; where low-close calls (calls that averaged 1.4 closing behaviors) had a success rate of approximately 70%. So, increasing close attempts actually proved to be 33% less effective.

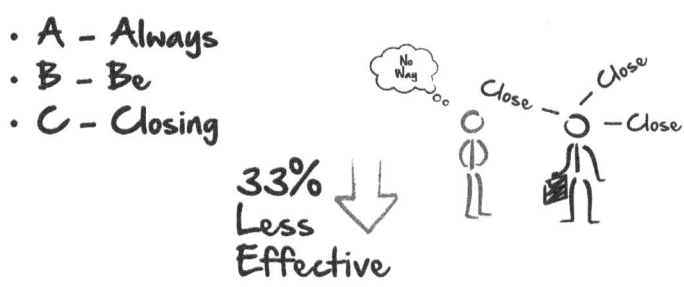

FACT: After the first attempt there is a negative correlation between closing frequency and sales call success.

Myth #3 – Closing Gambits Work on Both Large & Small Sales

Rackham tested the effect of closing on large and small sales and found that with small sales closing gambits actually improved sales by 4%. But, in large sales he discovered that closing gambits actually reduced sales by 9%.

What do you think the threshold is between large and small sales? At what dollar value does a small sale become large?

Amazingly, in his study, it was only $109.

If you happen to sell a lot of stuff below $109, maybe now is the time to whip out the double-reverse close. But for the rest of us the truth is closing gambits backfire.

FACT: Closing gambits become counter-productive above $109.

Myth #4 – Closing Gambits Show You Want the Business

This is obvious. The customer knows you want the business. The real question is: Do customers see closing gambits positively or negatively?

In a study of B2B buyers, six closing techniques were tested for their impact on buyer trust. Techniques tested were: Assumptive, Yes Set, Model/Example, Reciprocity, If-Then, and Impending Event.

In every case the sales technique proved to damage trust. And predictably, the most manipulative techniques damaged trust the most.

FACT: Closing gambits damage trust.

Myth #5 – Customers Are Happier After Making a Decision (so using closing gambits is actually helping them)

The logic seems to be: Clients are happier after they have made a decision, so manipulating or pressuring the client into a purchase is essentially for their own good.

I'm sure you recognize this as the-end-justifies-the-means thinking, and I'm sure it makes for great rationalization among some salespeople.

But, as it turns out, it is wrong.

How satisfied people are with decisions made under pressure happens to be an area well studied by social scientists. The studies show that the vast majority of people are very much less satisfied with decisions made under pressure. And, this is especially true with purchasing decisions.

This can have serious negative ramifications to your after-sale relationships and long-term success with clients. If you want to avoid buyer remorse, cancellations, and left-field complaints after the sale I recommend you avoid this thinking.

FACT: Customers are less satisfied with their decisions made under pressure.

Myth #6 – The Sale Will Close Itself

I fell for this myth when I first got into sales 30 years ago. With all this talk of how closing gambits don't work, you might conclude that you shouldn't attempt to close at all – and there are a few proponents of this mentality. But that's taking it too far.

Studies show that you must make an effort to advance the sale in order to be successful. Let's look at the data.

Surveys show that 50% to 90% of sales encounters (depending on industry) end without any commitment being asked for whatsoever.

Based on Rackham's research, asking just one closing question will increase your chances of advancing or closing the sale by 36%. Rackham says, "Traditional closing techniques are not the best way to obtain commitment from a customer in a major sale. But… as we've seen, doing nothing isn't effective either. The sale doesn't close itself."

The problem of not advancing the sale is much bigger than the problem of using closing gambits. You must make some effort to advance the sale. The sale will not close itself.

FACT: Sales don't close themselves. You must make an effort to advance or close the sale.

Myth #7 – Salespeople Fear Asking for Commitment

This last myth is actually a half-myth. Professionals don't fear asking for commitments so much as they fear damaging trust and rapport by appearing pushy.

When it comes to closing reluctance it's usually one of five issues:

1. The professional fears being pushy.
2. The professional fears being humiliated.
3. The professional fears being under-prepared.
4. The professional fears losing a closed sale.
5. The professional is ashamed to be in sales.

Half-Myth
People fear damaging trust & appearing pushy.

As mentioned earlier, the key to overcoming reluctance is to address the underlying issues and beliefs that are the source of the reluctance. We can make reluctance disappear by:

1. Placing a little thought into the way we ask, we can advance the sale without being pushy.
2. Crafting questions that make replies predictable, we eliminate risk of humiliation.
3. Keeping our questions simple and facilitative, there is no need to over-prepare.
4. Using an ingeniously designed query, each reply will advance the sale.
5. Selling with pure intent. Sales becomes a noble profession not worthy of shame when we see selling as service.

FACT: Addressing the underlying issues with closing eliminates fear and reluctance.

Myths and Facts of Closing

Myths	Facts
Myth #1 – Closing gambits work.	Closing gambits are negatively correlated with success and decrease sales. (in the 15% range)
Myth #2 – Always be closing.	Past the first attempt there is a negative correlation between closing frequency and sales call success.
Myth #3 – Closing gambits work on both large and small sales.	Closing gambits become counter-productive above $109.
Myth #4 – Closing gambits show you want the business.	Closing gambits damage trust.
Myth #5 – Customers are happier after making a decision. (so using closing gambits is actually helping them)	Customers are less satisfied with their decisions made under pressure.
Myth #6 – The sale will close itself.	The sale will not close itself. You must make an effort to advance or close the sale.
Myth #7 – Salespeople fear asking for commitment.	Addressing the underlying issues with closing addresses fear & reluctance.

CHAPTER 5

Planning = Success

Sales planning is strongly correlated with sales success. An international study of business-to-business sales teams found that the most effective sales groups (effectiveness being measured in terms of sales volume, market share, profitability, and customer satisfaction) were better at sales planning in all areas including: planning each sales call, planning sales strategies for each customer, planning coverage of assigned territory and customer responsibility, and planning daily activities.

Neil Rackham says, "A consistent finding about successful salespeople is that they put effort into planning. Good selling depends on good planning more than any other single factor."

Research shows that despite the correlation between planning and sales success, most sales people do not set realistic goals for themselves for each sales encounter.

Our objective in the next few chapters is to make you an excellent planner by:
- Describing what Sales Objectives and Call Objectives are
- Defining what makes a good Sales Objective and Call Objective
- How to set Call Objectives for each sales opportunity
- And most importantly, how to set up individual Call Objectives for each sales encounter

We will be staging each opportunity consistently and correctly so that each of your outcomes will always be improved.

EXERCISE #12 – Why Are You Engaging Your Client? - Part 1

Instructions: In the first column, write the names of five opportunities you are currently working. Then, answer this: "Why am I engaging this prospect at this time?"

Client/Prospect	Why am I engaging this prospect at this time?

Save your answers. We will return to this in a moment.

Do You Have Clarity?

The underlying principle behind all planning and goal setting is clarity. By being clear about what we really want from each opportunity and on each individual sales encounter, we set in motion conscious and unconscious forces that move us towards the achievement of our goals. It is important that we seek clarity about our objectives with each opportunity and each sales encounter.

It is also important that we distinguish between our overall sales objective and our individual call objectives on any given opportunity. Doing so gives us both the big picture of what we want to accomplish with our sale (the overall sales objective) and what we wish to accomplish on this particular call (the call objective).

When asked what their goal is for a given sales encounter, most salespeople reply with something like, "close the sale" or, "get the order." Unfortunately, in all but the simplest transactions the typical sales cycle will involve more encounters. Complex sales can exceed ten or more encounters. So, the idea that you are going to close the sale (as lofty as that goal may be) on any of the earliest encounters is completely unrealistic. Closing the sale is only a realistic accomplishment on the last call of the cycle.

Setting appropriate sales objectives for each opportunity and appropriate call objectives for each individual encounter will lead to an unbroken chain of successful advances that will ultimately lead to closing the sale and getting the order.

What's the Difference Between Sales Objectives & Call Objectives?

Sales objectives and call objectives have very specific criteria and knowing their criteria will make your use of The Perfect Close much more successful. For clarity, let us define here both sales objectives and call objectives.

Sales Objective - the revenue (or outcome) you anticipate generating by closing this particular opportunity with this particular client.

Call Objective - an advance or commitment that is the desired outcome of this particular sales encounter with this particular person or group.

The contrast here is that the sales objective is your ultimate goal of closing this specific *opportunity* while call objectives are our goals for achieving an advance on each particular sales call or *encounter*. The clearer these two are for you, the more rapidly you will reach your desired outcome.

How to Set Sales Objectives

It is common for people to be confused about their ultimate goal and the goal of their most immediate next step. By stripping away the clutter that may exist between the two, we can achieve clarity to give us perspective as well as the impulse to take the next best action.

Your overall sales objective defines the reason you are meeting with this particular prospect. The achievement of this objective could be six months away or as soon as the next encounter. If you don't have an overall sales objective when meeting with a client then you are, quite literally, meeting for nothing. There is no good reason for you to be there.

Your overall sales objective answers the questions, "What do I want to happen with this client that isn't happening now?" and "What do I ultimately want to happen at the conclusion of this opportunity?" Your answer to these questions should be specific and measurable.

A well-defined sales objective includes the following:
1. It is related to a specific product or service.
2. It is specific and measurable.
3. It has a specific target date for completion.
4. It should be realistic from the client's perspective.

Related to a specific product or service - Because it is a sales objective, it should be related to the specific product or service that you intend to sell to this particular client at this particular time. If you offer more than one product or service, then your objective should clearly state exactly which products and services are part of this particular objective. Related products and services can be bundled together into a single objective (i.e. a package). However, if you are engaged in offering more than one unrelated product or service to this prospective client, then you should have a separate sales objective for each specific product or service.

Specific and measurable - Your sales objective should specify the quantity of products or services that you intend to sell and their market value. For example, if it is licenses, then it will be the number of licenses you intend to sell; if it is service hours then it will be the number of hours; if it is for a term of service then it will be for a length of time (e.g. 36 months); and so on. When your objective is achieved it should be easy to measure the accomplishment. You should know, 1. If it was achieved or not, and 2. How close your objective was compared to what was actually sold.

Have a target date for completion - This is the likely timeframe for the completion of this specific sales objective. When do you expect that this sales objective will be accomplished? This timeframe should be realistic from the client's perspective.

Realistic from the client's perspective - All three of the previous criteria should be realistic from the client's perspective – not just yours. No wishful thinking here. No including products they are unlikely to buy. No astronomical quantities. No timeframes that would be impossible for the client to pull off. Everything should be realistic from the client's perspective based on what is happening for that client right now. Sometimes we do sell more than we expected and even sooner than we anticipated, but we want our sales objective to reflect what is realistic right now, and we can still hope and plan for the best.

For each sales objective you should be able to answer the following:
- The client I am engaging is...
- The product/service I am trying to sell is...
- The amount and value of the product/service I am trying to sell is...
- The date for this to be completed is...

Rephrased into a single sentence, it might look like this:

"I am engaging [client] with the intent to sell [amount] of [product/service] by [date]."

The main benefit to creating a sales objective for each opportunity is clarity. There is another major benefit, however. By creating sales objectives that meet all the important criteria (specific product, measurable, target date, and realistic) you will find that your sales forecast is much more accurate.

Sales Objectives Before You've Met with the Client

To create a realistic sales objective, you should have discovered some things about your prospective client. If you haven't had the opportunity to do discovery or haven't had much of a conversation with your prospective client yet, then:

Do what research you can prior to your next contact, and

Make discovery the objective of your next meeting.

You cannot ascertain what the solution (product, quantity, timeframe) should be or whether it is realistic without a discussion with your prospective client.

Prescription without diagnosis is malpractice. Once you have met with the client and determined the scope of their need, you can then craft your sales objective.

In some sales it is possible to have a reasonable idea of what the scope of the opportunity will be before you have met with the client. In this case you may have developed a value hypothesis and estimated a solution prior to having met. You may have even used this value hypothesis to engage the prospective client. If that is the case, just remember that these estimates are just that – estimates. Only after you have met with the client and determined the actual scope of their need is it appropriate to craft your sales objective.

EXERCISE #12 – Why Are You Engaging Your Client? - Part 2

Instructions: Using the five opportunities as in part 1 of this exercise, review your answer to why you are engaging each client to check if it has all four criteria of a Sales Objective (Product/Service; Quantity/Amt; Completion Date; Realistic to Client). Use the columns to the right to indicate if your description included that element.

Using the form below, revise your original Sales Objective, if necessary, to include all four criteria as indicated in the following model:

I am engaging [client] with the intent to sell [amount] of [product/service] by [date].

Adapt as necessary for your type of sale.

Client/Prospect	Product/Service	Qty. & Value	Completion Date
Sales Objective ☐ Realistic			
Sales Objective ☐ Realistic			
Sales Objective ☐ Realistic			
Sales Objective ☐ Realistic			
Sales Objective ☐ Realistic			

Look for patterns in your descriptions. Is there a pattern to any element that is missing? What needs to be added to make each one a complete sales objective.

Group Discussion: Break into groups of 3-4 and share your results. How do your results compare with others? Write the patterns you discover on a white board or flip chart. Share your observations with the group as a whole.

For many people, this is an eye-opening exercise the first time they perform it. What most professionals discover is that on average, they have only one or two of the four elements of a well-defined sales objective.

Because the sales objective is the foundation for the call objective (which is even more important), having a well-defined sales objective for each of your opportunities will make each of your individual sales encounters more effective.

Take the time to craft a well-defined sales objective for every opportunity that you are actively working.

🔑 **CLOSING SECRET** - Planning = Success

 **EXERCISE #13** – **Setting Sales Objectives for Your Opportunities**

Instructions: Using the Sales Objectives form on page 145 in the Free Additional Resources section of this book (download additional copies from PureMuir.com/TPCworkbook), create a sales objective for all your opportunities. Continue adding as time allows (these are real opportunities). Total your numbers accordingly to quantify the value of your pipeline. You might also consider creating a digital spreadsheet to facilitate this ongoing activity.

 Group Discussion: Break into teams of 3-4 and place the top two sales objectives for each person on a flip chart. Validate each sales objective as a group based on the criteria:

- Specific to product or service
- Measurable quantity
- Specific target date for completion
- Realistic from client's perspective

After vetting each sales objective total the number of sales objectives as well as the value of all the sales objectives at the bottom of the flip chart.

In the larger group, each team reviews one sales objective from their flip chart in the context of the four criteria and how it meets each criterion (particularly why it is realistic from the client's perspective).

Collect the flip charts with the top opportunities on them. Total the value of all the opportunities then place the flip chart pages on the wall where everyone can see them for the course of the workshop.

CHAPTER 6

The Critical Advance

It is very important to understand the difference between an advance, a continuation, and a close. Not knowing the difference between these three concepts can cause your sales to drag on and on in a never-ending state of non-closure.

Here are the definitions:

Close - a firm commitment to buy. It is the consummation of the sale and the final order that marks the transition from evaluating to actual ownership and use of the product or solution.

Advance - a significant action that requires energy by the client – either in the call or right after it – that moves the sale toward a decision.

Continuation - a situation where the sale will continue yet no specific action has been agreed upon by the customer to move forward.

There is an obvious demarcation when a close takes place, so it's clear when an opportunity becomes closed. However, even when we have a firm verbal commitment to buy, if paperwork or contracts are needed to complete the sale, the sale is not completed until the contracts are authorized by the client.

It's between the advance and the continuation that confusion typically sets in. Without a clear understanding of the difference between these two you will be doomed to potentially endless, time-consuming churn and needlessly long decision cycles. You will also be unsure about where you really stand in any given opportunity, which in turn, will cause forecasting issues.

It is quite common for professionals (even those dedicated strictly to selling) to misunderstand the differences between a sales advance and a continuation.

EXERCISE #14 – Advances & Continuations

Instructions: Review the list of Advances and Continuations below. In the second column label each one as either A for Advance or C for Continuation. In the "Strength" column rank just the Advances from 1-5 (1 weakest, 5 strongest).

	Advance / Continuation	"A" or "C"	Strength
1	Visit your booth at a trade show		
2	Say they like what they saw and will be in touch		
3	Attend a webinar		
4	Request references		
5	Ask a question that demonstrates they read some company material		
6	Compliments your demonstration		
7	Schedule a negotiation call		
8	Request a brochure		
9	Schedule a discovery		
10	Mention they know a user they respect		
11	Schedule a site visit		
12	Ask for technical information		
13	Agree to review a proposal with you		
14	You feel the relationship is strengthened		
15	Customer agrees to attend an off-site demonstration or meeting		
16	Ask for a demo		
17	Agree to run a trial or test of your product		
18	Ask for a project plan		
19	Engage in discussions with your technical team		

	Advance / Continuation	"A" or "C"	Strength
20	Ask for technical details		
21	Did an on-line demo on the website		
22	Say they will call you after the holidays		
23	Invite additional people to your presentation/demo		
24	Ask you to come visit next time you are in the area		
25	You discover they spoke with another customer		
26	Ask for an invite to an upcoming webinar		
27	Attend your company user-group meeting		
28	Ask for a whitepaper		
29	Review a proposal with you		
30	Ask for a copy of your PowerPoint		
31	Say they are extremely interested		
32	Call a reference		
33	Go to lunch with you		
34	Go with you on a site visit		
35	Golf with you		
36	Introduce you to another prospect		
37	Introduce you to a higher-level decision maker previously inaccessible to you		
38	Engage in negotiations		

 Group Discussion: Which actions would you rather see in your sales opportunities? Why is that?

When I first accepted a regional VP role, I met with each of my team members to review the opportunities they were working. One rep was absolutely convinced that he had a great opportunity on the line. The problem was, what should have been a relatively short sales cycle had gone on for almost a year. After reviewing this and other opportunities with him I decided to dig into what was happening during each contact with the prospective client. So, I would ask the rep to describe in detail what took place during his visit and the outcome. A pattern emerged as I listened to his replies:

- From an early contact, "They mentioned they know client XYZ and really respect them. I sent them literature."
- At an on-site visit, "I gathered a lot of great information."
- During an early encounter, "It was great. I did a demonstration, and they said they were really impressed."
- On another visit, "We did lunch, and I suggested she look at one of our whitepapers which I provided."
- On a phone call, "They asked me to come to the office next time I was in the area."
- Upon visiting, "They acknowledged that we have some really great stuff, and I offered them a sample project plan."
- Yet another contact, "We did a second demo over the web."
- A visit, "We did lunch and really strengthened our relationship."
- Later, "She thought maybe we should do another demo."
- Another visit, "I visited and collected some really useful information."
- And yet another call, "I asked them if they wanted a proposal and cost estimate, and they agreed."

On and on it went like this for nearly twelve months.

 EXERCISE #15 – What's Wrong Here?

Instructions: Before reading on, what patterns do you see in the list above? Which of these are Advances and which are Continuations? Are there similar patterns with how you defined the list in Exercise #14?

 Group Discussion: Discuss the patterns and in the outcomes of each of these sales encounters?

What's going on here? Are these not signs that we have an engaged prospective client? Barely. Here's why: Go back and review each response, but this time ask yourself, "What action did the client take during or after each contact?" Was the client investing any real energy in moving the project forward?

No. Beyond time spent at lunch and some visits, this client was not investing any real energy in moving forward. Here is where my rep went wrong – none of these are advances. They are all continuations.

An advance is a significant action that requires energy by the client – either during the call or right after it – that moves the sale toward a decision.

A continuation is a situation where the sale will continue, yet no specific action has been agreed upon by the customer to move forward.

My rep had completed a tremendous number of tasks while the client had performed none. And unfortunately, this rep's entire pipeline was filled with opportunities just like this one – all continuing endlessly; all going nowhere. Needless to say, it was affecting the rep's income in a negative way.

I continued probing the mindset of this rep by asking, "How do you know if a sales call has been successful? What tells you?"

His reply is very common among less experienced professionals. He said, "If they show interest, or if I improve the relationship or collect useful information."

"Hmm..., how can you tell if a client is interested?" I asked. He explained, "If they say they are interested or clearly show they are interested with their expression and body language."

I'll bet most people would agree with this statement, but if we use loose criteria like this, our sales calls will be doomed to potentially endless continuations and unnecessarily long sales cycles.

I asked, "What is your goal going into each sales situation?" He replied, "I only ask for a contract when they are ready, so my goal is usually to share some information with them, strengthen the relationship, or gather useful information."

Again, I'd wager that most people would agree that these are positive activities in the context of the sales cycle. Here's the problem – it's just not good enough.

What Is the Value of Your Time?

The only true asset anyone has is time. How we invest our time determines our happiness and success in relationships, business, and everything we do. The value we produce comes from the investment of our time. It is all we have. Therefore, it is critical that we invest it in the best ways possible.

> As professionals in any field (sales or otherwise) the only true asset we have is our time. How we invest our time determines our happiness and success in relationships, business, and everything we do.

Because my rep did not understand the difference between an advance and a continuation he was wasting a tremendous amount of time. Even worse, that lack of understanding was causing him to do things that actually lengthened his sales cycles. He was the source of his own problems. Ultimately, once he learned what you are about to learn regarding the differences between advances and continuations, he went on to be extremely successful.

Are You Efficient or Effective?

It's natural when attempting to improve our productivity that we immediately seek to do the things we already know, just faster. This is because we are drawing upon information within us – the processes we already know – as the basis for our improvement. We seek to do the things we know, just more efficiently.

My rep in the story above was already very efficient by any standard and pouring a ton of energy into his opportunities. Unfortunately, his energy was focused on doing the wrong things (and only very slightly so). Yet this slight difference was causing him to underachieve his potential in a very big way.

This then, is the difference between efficiency and effectiveness.

Efficiency is reducing the time it takes to do something.

Effectiveness is doing the right things.

Improving effectiveness requires assessing all the things we can do to produce results and adopting those things that produce the best outcomes. The challenge is, we don't know what we don't know. That is, we are not always aware of all the possible alternatives to the methods we are currently using. For this reason, improving effectiveness often requires help from someone with a perspective different than our own.

My rep was inadvertently seeking engagements that resulted in continuations. Once he understood this and learned how to instead create advances, his results improved dramatically.

Remember:

An **advance** is a significant action that requires energy by the client, either during the call or right after it, that moves the sale toward a decision.

A **continuation** is a situation where the sale will continue yet no specific action has been agreed upon by the customer to move forward.

The two critical elements in these definitions are action and energy.

Observing the action and energy a prospective client expends during or immediately following a meeting accomplishes two very important things:

1. It tells us just how engaged the prospect is.
2. It (potentially) moves the sales process one step closer to closure.

In general, the larger the sacrifice the client is willing to make to continue the process (i.e. energy expended), the better the indicator that they are serious about moving forward and, therefore, worth our investment of time.

> The larger the sacrifice the client is willing to make to continue the process, the better the indicator that they are serious about moving forward and, therefore, worth our investment of time.

My rep was never doing this. He was never really challenging his clients in a way that would test their commitment to change. On the contrary, he was actually volunteering to do work for them with little or no reciprocity on their side.

What does it tell us about the urgency a client feels when they are not willing to invest energy into the process?

What if his client had already independently completed an exhaustive assessment that went above and beyond what was needed and then documented it in a 30-page report? What would that tell us about their level of commitment?

This is what my rep was missing. By doing everything for the client, he learned nothing about the client's sense of urgency, nor their level of commitment toward finding a solution. By offering to do everything and never committing prospective clients to do anything he was missing out on an opportunity to gauge their commitment to the project. This was causing him to spend time on unqualified prospects. It was also virtually impossible for him to accurately forecast the likelihood of any opportunity coming to fruition.

There is nothing inherently wrong with offering to render free services to prospective clients to further a sales opportunity. However, this should be done with great caution because no client will turn down the value of a free service, if it requires no commitment on their own behalf. Without a clear understanding of when such a thing is actually advancing a sale you may fall into the same trap my rep did and invest a great deal of time in opportunities that will never pay off.

The Solution

How did we solve the problem? All it took was teaching my rep the difference between an advance and a continuation and getting him to make the objective of each call an advance. Once he accomplished this, the issue went away, and he more than doubled his sales from the previous year.

EXERCISE #16 – What Constitutes an Advance?

Instructions: Consider how you judge whether a given outcome of a sales encounter is an Advance or a Continuation? Write your thoughts below:

Group Discussion: In groups of 3 or 4 discuss your ideas and write them on a flip chart or white board. Each group chooses their best ideas to share with the larger group.

What Is the Acid Test for Advances?

The acid test for an advance is action and energy. By setting call objectives that require action and energy on behalf of your prospective client you will have a clear understanding of their commitment level while continually moving your sale toward closure.

If the client is not taking an action, it is not an advance.

If the action the client takes requires little to no energy, it is not an advance.

Examples of advances might include:
- Arrange for you to meet with a higher-level decision maker
- Agree to meet with your technical team and invest time to discuss requirements and options
- Share sensitive information needed for an assessment
- Arranging a group meeting with executives for you to review the details of your proposed solution face-to-face
- Have a meeting or conversation with a reference you provide

All these require both action and a decent amount of energy (or perhaps even personal risk in the case of the introduction).

There is a wide spectrum of possible advances in any given sale that range from very little commitment of time and energy to those requiring a great deal of commitment.

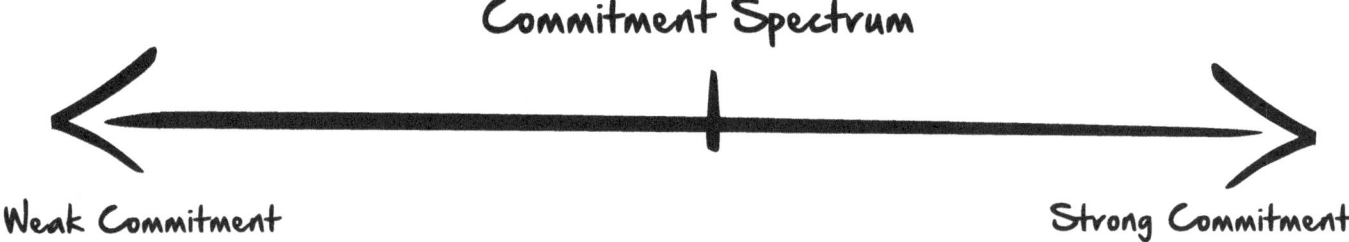

The key, then, is in the setting of our call objectives.

> The acid test for an advance is action and energy.

Recall what my rep answered when questioned about his goal for a typical call, "I only ask for a contract when they are ready, so my goal is usually to share some information with them, strengthen the relationship, or gather useful information."

Unfortunately, "sharing information," "strengthening the relationship," and "gathering information" are all continuations. None of these require much action or energy on behalf of the client. Every call provides the opportunity to share and gather information and improve the relationship. The problem with these types of objectives is that they lead to continuations not advances.

The solution for my rep was simply to set up true advances as primary and secondary objectives on each call. Before we discuss exactly how to do that, let us first discuss some of the psychology and science behind sales advances, and why they improve your sales outcomes.

The Science Behind Advancing the Sale

Two scientific concepts reveal why the practice of setting sales advances is so effective:

1. Commitment Consistency
2. Endowed Progress

Commitment Consistency

Once we have committed to an idea or goal, we are strongly compelled to honor that commitment to remain congruent with our self-image. Once committed, we convince ourselves that we have done the right thing and feel better about our decision by remaining consistent to it.

Once we accept small commitments, we become more willing to commit ourselves even further along those same lines. Our actions become increasingly consistent toward achieving the end goal.

This psychology is the first key to understanding why using advances to further our sales is so effective. Once a prospective client has agreed to take a step forward, there is a strong compulsion to remain consistent with the process and take an additional step, and another, and another. In this way each advance further increases the likelihood that our prospect will take another step in a chain of advances that lead to the ultimate conclusion of the sale.

Endowed Progress

The closer a prospect is to the end of the process the more committed they become to it. That is the essence of endowed progress.

Once we feel that we have made progress toward a goal we become even more committed toward continued efforts to achieve that goal. The closer we get to the goal, the more our effort increases.

You can think of this concept simply as closure. Once we set out to attain something (say the acquisition of a new solution or service, for example), the closer we get to completion, the more our efforts to do so accelerate.

Many things can be done to increase the client's perception of just how far along they are. And interestingly, studies indicate that the perception of progress is as effective as actual progress in getting clients to accelerate their efforts. That is the endowed part of endowed progress.

Making a client aware that they are closer to their goal than they may have realized and communicating to them how much progress they are making will accelerate their efforts toward closure.

A Virtuous Cycle

Commitment consistency and endowed progress are the two primary psychological reasons why utilizing sales advances is so effective in improving sales outcomes. Once the initial small advance (the commitment part) is achieved, clients are likely to take another second small step and so forth. Additionally, the more progress the client makes toward closure (the endowed progress part), the more accelerated their efforts become.

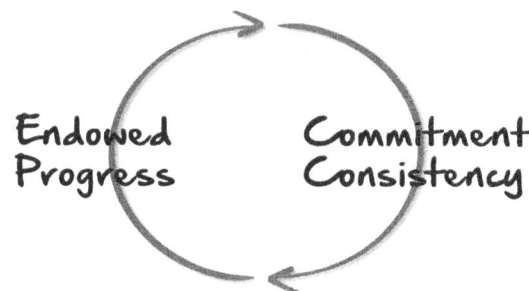

> *Commitment consistency and endowed progress are the two primary psychological reasons why utilizing sales advances is so effective in improving sales outcomes.*

Done correctly, these two principles of advancing the sale (commitment consistency and endowed progress) represent a virtuous cycle in which each component synergistically aids the other in ultimately closing the sale.

The key lies in the setting of our call objectives which is the subject of our next chapter.

🔑 **CLOSING SECRET** - Knowing the difference between an advance and a continuation can mean the difference between success and failure.

Conclusion

Understanding the distinctions between a continuation and an advance and why advances improve sales outcomes is integral to setting effective objectives for each sales interaction. Setting advances (rather than continuations) is key to making The Perfect Close work. Become proficient at setting advances as your primary and secondary objectives for each sales encounter, and you will dramatically increase your sales outcomes.

CHAPTER 7

How to Set Call Objectives

"The true goal for a salesperson is to help the customer win." –

Mike Weinberg

The way to achieve your ultimate Sales Objective is through the completion of incremental Call Objectives (Advances). By setting appropriate call objectives for each encounter we will achieve an unbroken chain of successful advances that will ultimately lead to closing the sale and getting the order.

> By setting appropriate call objectives for each encounter we will achieve an unbroken chain of successful advances that will ultimately lead to closing the sale and getting the order.

Incremental Advances are key to closing the sale.

EXERCISE #17 – Call Objectives - Part 1

Instructions: For each of the opportunities you selected in Exercise #12 - Part 2 on page 37, write what you were hoping to achieve on your most recent call with each client. Ignore the other columns for now, we'll come back to them. (If the opportunities listed in Exercise 12 no longer exist, feel free to use current ones.)

Client/ Prospect	What were you hoping to accomplish on your most recent call?	S/A	RCP	TA

It is very common for people to have difficulty articulating exactly what they are hoping to accomplish from sales calls. The attitude seems to be, "I'll just engage them and see what happens." This is just hoping, and hope is not a strategy.

These are some common mistakes made when setting call objectives:

1. The call objective is too general and not specific.
2. The call objective is unrealistic.
3. The call objective is not really an advance.

The Call Objective is too general - Call objectives should be specific and measurable. When the call objective is vague or general, it is easy to exit the encounter not really knowing whether the objective was achieved. Vague call objectives, such as "keep the momentum going," will leave you completely unclear about the direction you've gone and the progress you've made when the encounter is finished. Each call objective should be specific enough to easily determine at the end of the call whether it was accomplished.

The Call Objective is unrealistic - Initially when asked about their call objective, most professionals will say, "to close the deal." But, in all but the simplest transactions, actually closing the business is only realistic on the last step of the sale. It is also impractical to set call objectives that are farther along the sales cycle than the prospect is ready for now. For example, it's unlikely that your call will result in scheduling a site visit to a plant located on another continent before you have discussed your initial value proposition. Your call objective must be realistic from the client's perspective.

The Call Objective is not really an advance - Remember, an advance is a significant action that requires energy by the client, either during or immediately following the call that moves the sale toward a decision. That means that call objectives like, "demonstrate the ABC module," or "present XYZ…" are not advances, because they are not client-driven. Rather, the salesperson is thinking of what they (the salesperson) will do rather than what the client will do.

Setting a call objective that is not an advance is a very common pitfall. The acid test for an advance is action and energy. By setting call objectives that require both action and energy on behalf of our prospective client we will get a clear understanding of their commitment level while continually moving the sale toward closure.

EXERCISE #17 – Call Objectives - Part 2

Instructions: Return to your Form in Part 1. Complete the empty columns by marking a 'Y' if the objective is:

1. Specific & Measurable (S/M),

2. Realistic from Client Perspective (RCP)

3. A True Advance (TA)

For example, if your objective was indeed Specific & Measurable, place a "Y" under that column. If it was not, leave it blank.

Remember, a true advance must 1. Be client-focused (something the client does), 2. Require action & energy on the client's behalf, 3. Move the sale forward).

 Group Discussion: Break into groups of 3 or 4 and discuss your responses. Vet your answers and whether they meet the three criteria with the members of your group. Is there any pattern to the type of call objective you have been setting in the past? What changes or additions would make your call objectives more effective?

Amongst your group select a best and worst example and write it on a flip chart or white board. Take turns sharing these examples and what was learned with the entire group.

Until professionals receive training it is common for their call objectives to focus on what they, the professional, will do instead of what they want the client to do. Ignoring the client, their buying cycle, and considering only your own activities and sales cycle is one of the biggest mistakes in professional selling.

> *Ignoring the client, their buying cycle, and considering only your own activities and sales cycle is one of the biggest mistakes in professional selling.*

Here is the challenge it creates in relation to call planning: When you complete your planned action (giving a presentation, let's say) you tend to feel good about yourself, and your prospective client may even reflect this good feeling. This can blind you to assessing their true commitment level, since good feelings are not the acid test for an advance – only client action and energy are. And, because no action or commitment on behalf of the client has been given, we may leave the encounter thinking there is solid interest, when in fact, we have no real evidence of that.

Our job as professionals is not to educate or give presentations. Both of those are merely a means to an end. Our goal is to facilitate action on behalf of our clients. Always remember, we don't get paid for the actions we take. We only get paid based on the actions our clients take. The action we facilitate for our clients improves their condition as well as our own in a virtuous win-win cycle.

> *Our goal is to facilitate action on behalf of our clients.*

Embrace your role as a leader and change agent. Your prospect is meeting with you because they want to improve in some way, and they are looking to you for guidance and leadership. Through your knowledge, skills, and facilitation you become the catalyst that empowers them to reach their goals.

The actions that will best improve a client's condition will vary from client to client and will change over time. Therefore, we need to have a clear understanding of what constitutes a win for each specific client and articulate that in our overall sales objective.

As for individual call objectives, in a generic sense, every sales encounter has the same goal – to get the prospective client to commit to an advance and move closer to their desired outcome. In this sense you are a coach helping them get from where they are to where they want to be.

> *In a generic sense, every sales encounter has the same goal – to get the prospective client to commit to an advance.*

Coming up we will explore an entire range of advances from best to worst that you might set as your call objective – so you have a targeted ideal advance as well as several fallback advances if your ideal advance proves unrealistic.

The Three Magic Pre-Call Questions

As we conclude this chapter, I want to introduce you to the Three Magic Pre-Call Questions. You should know the answer to each of these before going into any sales encounter. If you do nothing more than master the habit of answering these three questions before every sales encounter, you will find your effectiveness in sales magnified many times over. This habit alone will make this workbook worth 10,000 times what you paid for it.

Here are the Three Magic Pre-Call Questions:

Prior to every sales encounter – whether in person, by phone, or otherwise – answer the following three questions:

1. Why should this client see me?
2. What do I want the client to do?
3. How can I provide value on this encounter?

EXERCISE #18 – **The Three Magic Pre-Call Questions - Part 1**

Instructions: Look at your calendar and write down your next five appointments. For each appointment, write your answer to the three questions. Disregard the scores (we will complete those in the next chapter).

Client Appointment	Why should this client see me?	What do I want the client to do?	How can I provide value on this encounter?
1	Score: ___	Score: ___	Score: ___	Score: ___
2	Score: ___	Score: ___	Score: ___	Score: ___
3	Score: ___	Score: ___	Score: ___	Score: ___
4	Score: ___	Score: ___	Score: ___	Score: ___
5	Score: ___	Score: ___	Score: ___	Score: ___

What did you discover? Was it easy, or did you find it challenging? After getting this far, most folks can do a decent job of answering the second question (though we will greatly improve on that shortly). However, all three questions can throw people for a loop. In the upcoming chapters, we will discuss each question individually with our main focus being the second question and briefly touching on questions one and three.

> *Answering the three magic pre-call questions before each encounter will magnify your effectiveness many times over.*

These preliminaries are important to be able to execute The Perfect Close to its maximum effectiveness.

🗝 **CLOSING SECRET** - By setting appropriate call objectives for each encounter, we will achieve an unbroken chain of successful advances that will ultimately lead to closing the sale.

Conclusion

Call Objectives (pre-planned advances) are a key part of maximizing the effectiveness of The Perfect Close. For that reason, the next three chapters discuss the three magic pre-call questions in more detail. Having preplanned advances as your call objectives will multiply your effectiveness many times over. Planning your call can be simple. By answering the three magic questions you will be prepared to use The Perfect Close and further increase your effectiveness on each encounter.

In the next chapter we will explore one of the most important elements of your planning process – the answer to the first of the three magic pre-call questions: Why should this client see me?

CHAPTER 8

Why Should This Client See Me?

"The only person that can decide what is valuable... is the customer."

– John Spence

EXERCISE #18 – The Three Magic Pre-Call Questions - Part 2

Instructions: Individually or in a group, review your answers in Exercise #18 Part 1 on page 53 and honestly judge how compelling and effective each answer is on a scale from 1 (weak) to 5 (strong). Total those scores and write that number in the Client Appointment box. How many appointments total 15?

Group Discussion: What benefits and challenges do you find in answering these questions? Amongst your group select a best and worst example and write it on a flipchart or whiteboard. Take turns sharing these examples and what was learned with the entire group.

Why Should This Client See Me?

This question gets right to the core of your value proposition. Something you offer brings measurable value to your clients. What is it? The measurable value you bring to your clients is the reason they should meet with you. That is your Value Proposition.

It is common for salespeople and other professionals to not have a clear understanding of their value proposition and the value they bring to their clients. Unfortunately, your value proposition is mission-critical information that you must have to succeed in selling. It is vital that you have a clear understanding and can articulate in a tangible way the value you bring your customers.

> *The measurable value you bring to your clients is the reason they should meet with you. That is your Value Proposition.*

Developing your value proposition is a large and important topic and beyond the scope of this workbook. A future work will address how to develop and best articulate your value proposition to clients in detail. For now, just in case you found yourself without a clear value proposition, we offer this short bit of coaching. If you are experienced in this area, skip to the next chapter.

Communicating Your Value Proposition

A value proposition is the measurable value you deliver to your clients. This is the reason why they should meet and do business with you. As we've seen, most people tend to describe what they do rather than the value they bring. This is a big mistake. It is critical that you are able to articulate the real value you deliver.

Your value proposition communicates not only the measurable value you deliver, but also how you differ from competitors or product alternatives. Without a measurable value proposition, it will be hard for you to command any price for your solution because prospective clients will have no discernible value to compare against your price. Without a value proposition your product or service simply looks like an additional cost.

Lack of a value proposition also tends to make all vendors look the same to buyers. In the absence of a value proposition, clients will assume that all solutions in the same space solve with roughly the same degree of effectiveness. How can they know otherwise? A strong value proposition is among the most important things you can develop for your business.

> *A strong value proposition is among the most important things you can develop for your business.*

A basic value proposition has three core components:

1. A Metric 2. A Direction 3. Magnitude

Metrics - The metric component is the name attached to the area(s) you improve. All businesses have them. Sometimes they are formalized, and sometimes they are not. It answers, "How do you measure whether or not you are doing well in this area?"

Examples of formalized Metrics within Sales might include:

- Number of Units Sold
- Close Ratio
- Revenue Growth
- Lead Conversion Ratio
- Number of Opportunities

Examples of formalized Metrics within Accounts Receivable might include:

- Days Sales Outstanding (DSO)
- Percentage of AR over 60 Days
- Average Days Delinquent
- Bad Debt Percentage
- Operating Cost per Transaction

Every industry has formalized metrics for measuring performance.

Sometimes metrics are less formal than the above examples, but rest assured they are still there. Very often, they are simply measured in terms of time, money, counts, ratios, or percentages. Other times the metric will be something unique to that customer alone.

Some examples might be:

- Time to Complete (something)
- Customer Satisfaction
- Acceptance Rate
- Positive Comments
- Usability
- Quality

> *Every industry has formalized metrics for measuring performance.*

You can discover the metric(s) your clients use to measure performance by asking these questions:
- "What tells you when you are doing well in this area?"
- "What tells you if something is going wrong?"
- "What suggests to you that you could be doing better in this area?"

With metrics, you are simply looking for the means by which they measure results (good or bad). When you use a client's metrics in your value proposition you are speaking their lingo and communicating on a level they immediately understand. Simply using their terms will increase both your value and your credibility.

EXERCISE #19 - Your Industry Metrics

Instructions: List 3 solutions (products/services) that your company offers and write them below. For each solution, write the metrics that answer these questions (if possible, brainstorm this exercise as a group):

- "What metric indicates you are doing well in this area?"
- "What alerts you if something is going wrong?"
- "What suggests that you could be doing better in this area?"

Use metrics referenced in this chapter, if desired.

Solution 1	Solution 2	Solution 3
Positive Metric Indicators:		
Warning Metric Indicators:		
Improvement Metric Indicators:		

Group Discussion: For each solution, circle the three metrics that are the best indicators for improvement for your clients and/or showcase the measurable value you bring. Share your metric choices with the large group and describe why you chose them.

NOTE: If you are not already tracking these metrics for each of your clients, begin doing so now. Discover these values before the sale and monitor them over time. When you do this, you will have case study metrics for every client and feedback that is invaluable for both you and your client.

Direction - Direction is simple. It answers the question, "What is happening to the value of this metric?" Is it going up or down? Depending on the context, either one might be good. We want Sales Revenue to go up, and we want Material Costs to go down – both are good.

Magnitude - Lastly, we have magnitude. Magnitude answers "How much...?" That is, how much is the metric going up or down? What is the actual value of the change? Did it go up or down by a percentage? Was it reduced by a fixed amount? What is the quantified level of improvement?

> *When you use a client's metrics in your value proposition you are speaking their lingo and communicating on a level they immediately understand.*

Putting Your Value Proposition Together

With these three components you have the minimum you need to craft a value proposition. The components can be arranged in various ways to maximize clarity and impact. Here is a basic formula and example:

Formula: [Direction] + [Metric] + [Magnitude]

> *Direction + Metric + Magnitude = Value Proposition*

Examples & Variations:

- We increase lead conversion by an average of 47%.
- We reduce DSO (Days Sales Outstanding) on average 21%.
- We improve close ratios per rep an average of 29%.
- Time-to-market is reduced on average over 50%.
- First pass clean claim rate is improved to 99% on average.
- Denials are on average reduced to less than 1%.

EXERCISE #20 - Crafting Value Propositions

Instructions: If possible, break into groups of 3 or 4. Using the three elements of a basic value proposition (Direction, Metric & Magnitude), craft a value proposition for each of your top metrics from the previous exercise. (If you had 3 solutions with 3 metrics each, you should have 9 value propositions.) Use real data so you have actual, usable value propositions at the end of this exercise. If you do not have real data available, make it a priority to begin collecting that data immediately.

Number your final value propositions in descending order of impact (most impactful first). If working in a group, write the best on a flip chart or whiteboard.

Solution 1	Solution 2	Solution 3

Group Discussion: Share your value propositions with the entire group. Discuss which value proposition you feel is most compelling and why you placed it highest in your list.

This is the bare minimum. There are many other elements that go into creating an effective value proposition such as target statements and impacts. You should have a value proposition for every solution and service, so you can speak confidently about the value each one brings. Additionally, you will probably need a more generalized value proposition that encompasses everything your business offers. A full treatment of how to develop value propositions is beyond the scope of this work, but at the completion of this chapter you will have foundational value propositions to use in your sales and marketing messaging.

With your value proposition(s) crafted, you will be able to easily define a legitimate business reason to meet with your prospective client. That's your answer to, "Why should this client see me?"

Now it's time to work this into a complete sentence for your sales encounter and include what you know about the client's current situation. Here's an example:

Question: Why should this client see me?

Answer: This client should see me because with their new expansion it is likely I can reduce their human resource costs as much as 19% using automation.

EXERCISE #21 - Applying Your Value Proposition to Your Upcoming Appointments

Instructions: Refer to your five upcoming appointments used in Exercise #18 Part 1 on page 53. Using your newly developed value propositions and what you've learned thus far, rewrite your answers to "Why should this client see me?"

Client Appointment	Why should this client see me?	What do I want the client to do?	How can I provide value on this encounter?
1 Score: ___	 Score: ___	 Score: ___	 Score: ___
2 Score: ___	 Score: ___	 Score: ___	 Score: ___
3 Score: ___	 Score: ___	 Score: ___	 Score: ___
4 Score: ___	 Score: ___	 Score: ___	 Score: ___
5 Score: ___	 Score: ___	 Score: ___	 Score: ___

Group Discussion: Break into groups of 3 or 4 and share your revised answers. Have each member of the group select their top revision and write it on a flipchart or whiteboard. Share these answers with the entire group.

🔑 **CLOSING SECRET** - Your value proposition is mission-critical information that you must have to succeed in selling.

Conclusion

Your Value Proposition communicates the tangible results you produce for your clients, differentiates you from competitors and alternatives, and justifies your pricing.

Creating a value proposition for your business as well as each of your solutions represents foundational work that must take place before value can be communicated in any form of messaging.

Your value proposition answers "Why should this client see me?" in a compelling and tangible way. Clarity in your value proposition will magnify both your value and credibility with prospective clients. It will also direct and accelerate your conversations with clients right to the core reasons for doing business with you.

In the next chapter we will discuss how to answer the second of the three magic pre-call questions: What do I want the client to do?

CHAPTER 9

What Do I Want My Prospective Client to Do?

*"There are a lot of smaller 'asks' that you need to make on your way to the final 'ask.'
You can't move the final 'ask' forward by skipping the 'asks' that should have come before it."*

– Anthony Iannarino

The answer to "What do I want my client to do?" is the basis of your call objective – the advance you want to happen as a result of this encounter. It is the action you want them to take. Each advance will incrementally bring you and your client to an arrangement that benefits you both.

You already understand that an advance requires both action and energy on behalf of your prospect. Now, let's develop a range of possible advances for all your sales encounters. By doing this, you will have an ideal advance to work toward as your call objective plus several fallback advances, if your ideal advance proves unrealistic for some reason.

Ideal Advance - the highest level of commitment you can reasonably expect your prospect to make as a result of this encounter.

Ultimately, the ideal advance on any given sales encounter would be to close the business. However, as previously mentioned, that is only occasionally a reasonable outcome in a complex sales process that involves more than one call. For that reason, we will be aiming for the highest level of incremental commitment we can realistically achieve.

There will generally be many potential actions that a prospect can take to move the sale forward. What we want to do is make the most of our time and the prospect's time by facilitating the largest incremental commitment appropriate at this juncture. To do that we will need to evaluate our possible advances against each other. The four criteria of call objectives will make that easier.

Call objectives require four criteria. They should:
1. Be specific and measurable.
2. Center on the action the prospect will take.
3. Move the sale forward.
4. Be reasonable from the prospect's perspective.

Specific and measurable - Just like sales objectives, call objectives should be specific and measurable. In the case of call objectives, it is considerably easier because we are looking for tangible evidence that the action took place. It is simply an action or commitment made by your prospect. So, it either happened or it didn't. Changes in attitude or feeling are challenging to measure. So instead, look for actions that demonstrate their change in attitude or feeling. As you brainstorm advances ask, "What actions demonstrate a change (or confirmation) of attitude or feeling?"

Center on the action the prospect will take - We've covered this, but it bears repeating. Call objectives are about what we want the *prospect* to do – not what *you* do. As we brainstorm all the possible advances, remember to focus on actions your prospect could take as a result of your meeting. Ask yourself, "What action could my prospect take to advance the sale forward?"

Move the sale forward - Each advance should incrementally progress the sale toward ultimate completion. Depending on circumstances, there may be many increments or just a few. The key here is that, at the minimum, each action should add some sort of momentum to the sales process. Not all actions taken by the prospect will move the sale forward. Meetings, for example, neither move the sale forward nor backward. They are neutral. What happens as a result of the meeting may advance your sale, but the meeting itself is simply an opportunity.

Be reasonable from the prospect's perspective - As you brainstorm potential advances, your list of possible prospect actions should range from simple to almost impossible. I once had a rep suggest that an entire client site attend a national user's conference. While an excellent thought exercise, it was impractical for the client to shut down operations for a week so their entire group could attend our user's conference. Still, once we pared it down to a reasonable scope, this was an excellent suggestion for advancing the sale. In the end, a dozen members of their staff attended the conference, and it contributed to garnering a multi-million-dollar account.

EXERCISE #22 – What Do I Want My Client to Do?

Instructions: Return to Exercise #21 on page 61 and answer "What do I want the client to do?"

Then, break into groups of 3 or 4 and review your answers. Using the four criteria for a Call Objective (1. specific & measurable, 2. center on action the prospect will take, 3. move the sale forward, 4. be reasonable from the prospect's perspective) have each member of the group score the quality of your answers on a scale from 1 (weak) to 5 (strong). Average the group's scores and write that score in the lower-right-hand corner of that answer. If working solo, score your own answers.

 Group Discussion: As a group discuss your answers and what you find good and what you find challenging in answering this question. Then, amongst your group select a best and worst example and write it on a flipchart or whiteboard. Take turns sharing these examples and what was learned with the entire group.

Advances vs. Engagement

There are many interactions that are generally positive but do not technically qualify as advances because they don't represent commitment, or they lack the sufficient energy required to be advances. Before brainstorming possible advances, we should understand the distinction between an advance and what I deem sales *engagement*.

Sales Engagement - interest that does not involve obligation.

This practical definition gives us a useful way to differentiate between an advance and what is simply curiosity or interest on behalf of a client. An advance involves a commitment or obligation of some kind, yet there are many interactions with clients that don't involve commitments or obligations but do demonstrate genuine curiosity and interest.

Sales Engagement – Interest that does not involve obligation.

One way to approach engagement versus an advance is to consider them on a priority scale. On one end of the scale engagement represents items that are of interest but not yet enough of a priority to invest time and energy, and on the other end of the spectrum you have advances which are of high enough priority to take action on.

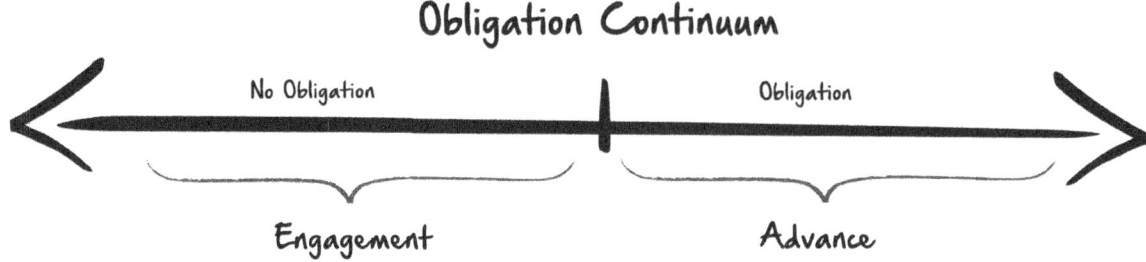

This helps to gauge:

1. The prospective client's level of commitment.
2. The best possible advance to suggest at this moment in time.

This allows you to make the best use of both the prospect's time as well as your own.

The trap professionals fall into is wasting huge amounts of time on prospective business that will never close because they have misjudged curiosity and interest (and sometimes simple politeness) as indicators of good sales opportunities. Curiosity and interest are nice, but we don't want to make it more than it is – and we certainly don't want to invest our most valuable resource (time) without a reasonable assurance of a positive outcome.

EXERCISE #23 – Sales Engagement For Your Type of Sale

Instructions: In groups of 3 or 4, or individually, brainstorm types of customer interest that do not involve obligation for your type of sale. Write your answers below.

 Group Discussion: Share your answers with the whole group and collect the top ideas on a flipchart or whiteboard..

Common Indicators of Engagement Often Confused for Advances

- Prospect asks you for a proposal. This is a small sign of engagement – commonly mistaken as an advance. Prospects, even disinterested ones, want to know prices. So, expect them to request a proposal which, in most cases, is better than you suggesting it since the timing and context of their request will reveal something about where they are in the sales process.

The problem is their request doesn't require any energy or commitment from them. Instead, upgrade this to an advance by suggesting something logical of them that requires a commitment or expenditure of energy, such as a detailed assessment or discovery before you produce the proposal.

- You send a proposal. Sending a proposal is engagement, not an advance. And, doing so haphazardly via email is a bad idea. When you email an undirected proposal you lose the opportunity to:

1. Review, clarify, and confirm the accuracy of the proposed solution,
2. Collaborate with the prospect to make the proposal perhaps bigger or even more ideal,
3. Discuss dynamics around what will happen next, and
4. Further develop your relationship with the prospect.

A common excuse by those who confess to simply emailing proposals is that the prospect has stopped responding to calls and messages – probably because there's been no value inherent during their interactions. If you are not adding value or insight to every interaction, why should the prospect bother? Furthermore, once they have your proposal, they may decide they have everything of value that you can offer and will only reach out on their terms.

Never send a proposal if you can deliver and review it face-to-face. If that's not an option, schedule an online meeting to deliver and review your proposal with them. Then, you will have an advance.

- Prospect asks questions regarding the proposal or solution. Asking specific, detailed questions is a good sign of engagement since the quality of their questions reveals interest and careful consideration. Interest is not commitment, however. Use the information you glean from their questions to suggest a logical advance that will move the process incrementally forward as well as test their commitment to the process.

- Prospect reads or studies your presentation or support materials. When significant time and energy is invested reviewing your presentation or support materials, it is a positive sign representing worthwhile engagement and possibly an advance. The challenge is in deciphering how much time and energy the prospect actually invested. If you can tell by their questions and comments that they have truly pored over your materials, great! They have demonstrated engagement. More often, however, prospects request these documents (or simply accept them at your suggestion) and never actually do anything with them.

Instead, turn their interest into a meeting or conversation and suggest a logical advance as an outcome of that.

- One of their personnel contacts you to gather additional information (IT, engineers, managers, supervisors). Be encouraged if a member of your prospect's staff suddenly contacts you for additional information. This most likely, though not always, indicates an advance has taken place internally, without your knowledge. These requests come from staff likely to be affected by the purchase, but that doesn't necessarily mean they support it. Nevertheless, it definitely represents engagement.

The best approach: engage the person in a helpful dialogue about their role in the process, their feelings about the project, and the dynamics around the decision. Their answers will tell you if they are friend or foe. Then, convert this interaction into an advance by committing them to gathering agenda items for a group meeting, attending a reference client visit, etc.

- Contact requests help explaining a detail of the sale to another person. A prospect requesting advice about how to present your solution to others is engagement that foreshadows a possible advance. The risk is they aren't likely to articulate the value of your solution better than you. Upgrade this engagement to an advance by scheduling a meeting with the other person(s) to deliver the explanation yourself. If their internal politics dictate otherwise, discuss the dynamics of the situation with your prospect to understand what they are trying to accomplish and assess the best way to achieve that for them.

- Prospect attends a webinar or watches an online demo. When a prospect or someone in their organization does this or another similar activity, it demonstrates a good level of engagement, but these information-gathering activities generally don't require a high level of energy or commitment. Be aware these activities could be antagonistic as they may be gathering information against the project. If this occurs toward the end of your sales cycle, it may indicate that the prospect is not as far along as you thought.

The best course of action – contact the person who took these actions and engage them further to understand their motives. Learn the situation and dynamics involved, then with that knowledge, suggest one of your advances.

- Contact refers another prospect to you. This shows a very high level of engagement, and if they've already contacted the referral and had a discussion about your solution, then congratulations! You have an advance. If, however, they are simply dropping the name of a possible prospect, you need to dig deeper.

Discover the details behind their relationship with the referral and understand why they are suggesting it. Then, upgrade this engagement to an advance by asking if they are willing to make the introduction for you.

You now know the difference between an advance and engagement and how to avoid mistaking them. This knowledge is critical to continuing momentum in your opportunities. With the Perfect Close you will suggest an advance, and the actions we suggest must genuinely move the client toward their goals. With this in mind, it's time to brainstorm possible advances for your type of sale.

Brainstorming Advances

This is a critical exercise because these advances will form the basis of the questions you will ask using the Perfect Close. The strategy is to give yourself a wide range of possible actions that your prospective client might take.

Before starting, note that every sale is unique and advances that work wonderfully for one opportunity might be inappropriate for another. In fact, to the degree that you are tailoring your advances for a given opportunity, it is a good sign that you are genuinely engaging your prospect at a higher level. So, this exercise should be performed before each sales encounter to help you think through the best possible outcome for that prospect at that time. For now, we will be performing this exercise in a generic sense for all opportunities.

You'll find that for your type of sale, there will be a pattern to the kinds of advances you can reliably request with positive results. Brainstorming those now will speed the process for you in the future and possibly help you discover some advances that you may not have considered before.

If you are on a sales team, this exercise is best done as a group where you can brainstorm together and bounce ideas off one another. To facilitate that process, download additional copies of this form, and others, at PureMuir.com/TPCworkbook

EXERCISE #24 - Brainstorming Advances

Instructions: In groups of 3 or 4, or individually, brainstorm all the possible actions your prospects could take and list them under Possible Advance/Client Action.

Then, under Measured By - write how you will know when this action has taken place. This will discern advances from engagement or mere feelings.

Under Impact - rate how impactful each advance would be on the development of your sale (H-high, M-medium, L-low, N-none). This will identify your most ideal advances.

Viability - rate the likelihood of achieving each advance from 1 (difficult) to 5 (easy). This will assess how realistic each advance is from your client's perspective. (These ratings would differ depending on the client, but for now think broad sense.)

Priority - if you were planning for an actual encounter, you would prioritize each advance here. For now, we are simply brainstorming so you can skip that column.

Your table should look similar to this.

Possible Advance/ Client Action	Measured By	Impact	Viability	Priority
Get introduced to executive management	Introduction takes place	H	4	
Agree to do assessment & share financials	Shares financials, schedules assessment	H	2	
Arrange meeting with technical team to discuss requirements/options	Technical meeting takes place	M	3	
Meet with reference account	Reference account meeting takes place	M	3	
Schedule demonstration	Demonstration takes place	L	5	

Possible Advance/ Client Action	Measured By	Impact	Viability	Priority	Strengthen

 Group Discussion: Share brainstormed advances and collect all answers into a master list for future reference.

Building on Your Possible Advances

Many find this exercise illuminating, and no doubt you discovered some patterns to the advances and action steps that you most often use. From here we can build on that.

The best salespeople get prospects to agree to a continuous stream of small actions. These ingenious actions, forged from the creativity of these skilled professionals, can be amazing. They always have an ideal advance as well as an array of alternate actions to propose. This increases the likelihood that each encounter will end with one or more advances.

> *The best salespeople are able to get prospects to agree to a continuous stream of small actions.*

Tips for Strengthening Your Advances

By simply tweaking your advances, you can increase their effectiveness to a large degree. Make your advances stronger by considering the following tips.

- **Make your interaction as direct and personal as possible.** With the advent of the internet there are many efficient and time-saving ways to interact with your prospects and clients that do not involve face-to-face contact (e.g. email, internet presentations, conference calls, etc.), but efficient is not always effective. Communication, understanding, and the development of relationships are all maximized in face-to-face interactions. You cannot detect facial cues on conference calls and internet presentations.

To the degree that you can be directly engaged in personal, face-to-face interactions with your prospects, the strength and effectiveness of your advances will be improved. In-person, face-to-face interactions are the best.

- **Pick the best possible location for your meeting.** Venue affects meeting dynamics and, to a large degree, can make a meeting more or less effective. The outcomes are situational and require some consideration:

- Reference Client's Site - Arranging to meet a prospect at an existing client's (aka reference client) location could greatly increase the effectiveness of your meeting. This environment should be oozing social proof, and your prospect will have direct access to an existing client for third-party validation of your solution.
- Event or Show - This can help or hurt depending on circumstances. Trade show meetings can be convenient for prospects, but potential distractions and the proximity to competitors and alternate choices can cause issues. Still, such events often create excitement and high-energy levels that can motivate prospects. If it's your own event (like a user-group meeting), you have a meeting trifecta: heightened energy, access to your top personnel, and social proof all around you. Either way, plan your meeting carefully to minimize distractions.
- Your Corporate Office - This is a great way to showcase the leadership of your management team as well as the talent of your technical, implementation, and support teams. Meeting here will help address questions regarding your company's credibility, competency, or capabilities to solve or execute the solution. A well-choreographed visit to your headquarters can strengthen your advance significantly.
- The Prospective Client's Site - Meeting at the prospect's location is far stronger than an internet-based meeting or phone conference and will greatly improve the interaction. However, this site may also come with potential interruptions. If that's a real possibility, it may make sense to meet off site.
- Off-site Location - The benefit of meeting off site is to eliminate interruptions and allow prospects to focus on your message and the task at hand. But, off-site meetings can vary wildly in their scope and effectiveness – a dedicated retreat to a foreign destination can create maximum impact but may be impractical; a simple meal off site can be a mixed bag. Off-site meetings eliminate the opportunity to add additional parties or explore either their or your premises. Accomplish an onsite and off-site meeting in the same encounter with a tour of their premises and then a lunch meeting. Plan off-site meetings strategically to insure a good quality meeting.

- **Add valuable people to your meeting.** Involving key people either from your company or the prospect's, like decision makers, technical resources, domain experts, or even existing clients, may be an advance in itself. And, this can strengthen not only your meeting but also its resulting action items and advances.

- **Add value to every interaction.** Strengthen every encounter by adding value in some way. By making each meeting inherently worthwhile, you train your prospects and clients to value every interaction with you. There are many ways to achieve this. This is the subject of our next chapter.

EXERCISE #25 - Strengthen Your Advances

Instructions: If possible, reconvene into your original small groups. Review your answers in Exercise #24 on page 69, and using the Tips suggested above, select one (or create your own) that would strengthen each advance. Write them in the Strengthen column.

Group Discussion: Each group shares their ideas for strengthening advances with the entire group. These ideas are added to the master list.

Additional Resources

If you are interested in creating even more advances for your call objectives download the forms and documents at PureMuir.com/TPCworkbook. There you will find many additional ideas on how to develop effective advances for your type of sale.

CLOSING SECRET - By brainstorming we can plan the ideal advance as well as alternate/additional advances for our sales encounter.

Conclusion

Complex sales are like a flywheel. Each time we obtain an advance from a prospect the flywheel gains momentum. Some sales require many pushes on the flywheel and others just a few. By brainstorming and planning ahead we can choose the ideal advance for our interaction and have a number of alternate advances in the event our primary call objective proves unrealistic.

Your ideal advance is the highest-level commitment you can reasonably expect your prospect to make as a result of this encounter.

Each successful advance adds momentum to your sale's flywheel and brings your client closer to their goal. As mentioned, planning your call is a big factor in sales success. Next, we'll step through how to plan calls that deliver value and advance the sale.

Notes:

CHAPTER 10

How Can I Provide Value on This Encounter?

"Value doesn't happen by accident. It is the result of deliberate planning and preparation."

- Andy Paul

Whenever I conduct training I like to start with what I call a "workout" session – where I ask my team what their top challenges are.

Can you relate to some of these?

- After working with customers for some time, they suddenly go silent. Usually right after giving them a proposal.
- Prospects reach out and show interest, but they just don't engage – despite stated interest.
- After progressing steadily through the process, the prospect suddenly goes with a competitor.
- The customer chooses a clearly inferior solution.
- 14 million salespeople are predicted to lose their jobs in the next few years, will I be one of them?
- I'm working hard, but how can I sell more?

Certainly, there are others, but all of these suffer the same root cause and can be remedied by making one simple change.

The Three Magic Pre-Call Questions

We have answered two of the Three Magic Pre-Call Questions:

- Why should this client see me?
- What do I want the client to do?

Now, for the final important question, "How can I add value on this encounter?"

What follows reveals why it is critical that we add value on every single customer encounter as well as helpful guidelines, tips, and exercises on how to do so.

> *It is critical that we add value on every single customer encounter.*

The Disappearing Sales Process

Adding value is a relatively new development in selling. Prior to the widespread use of the Internet, salespeople rarely needed to deliver anything beyond information about their products and services. Now, all that information is readily available online. Search engines locate exactly what buyers are looking for in fractions of a second. And, thanks to very sophisticated algorithms, most of the vital information is likely to be contained in the first few pages of results.

Research conducted by the Corporate Executive Board reveals that on average customers complete 57% of their buying process before ever contacting a salesperson. Gartner Research predicts that in a few years, 85% of business interactions will be executed without human intervention. These are game-changing dynamic for millions of salespeople worldwide to which we must adjust. Bringing added value is that adjustment.

So, today's buyers have two options:
1. Bypass a salesperson and do business transactionally, or
2. Engage a sales professional to derive value from the sales experience.

As more and more purchasers choose option one, the bar of expectation for what salespeople should deliver through the sales process is raised for buyers who choose option two.

I can't overstate the impact of this new dynamic. Delivering value on each and every sales encounter is about staying relevant to the buyer. Without it, they no longer need you. We must make it imperative to add value on every sales interaction.

🗝 **CLOSING SECRET** - Every sales interaction must be inherently valuable.

You Are the Biggest Factor

Many studies over the years have examined which sales factors are most influential in the buying process. Two noteworthy and extensive studies from HR Chally and the Corporate Executive Board spanned more than 20 years and exceeded 100,000 interviews. Examining many factors including company and brand, quality of offering, total solution, total value, the salesperson, and price, they both determined that, by far, the most influential factor is the salesperson. In fact, the salesperson is two to four times more important than any other factor.

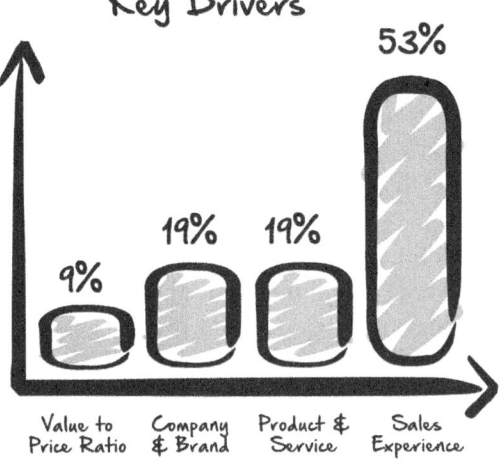

I'd like to accentuate three conclusions from this data:
1. You cannot rely solely on your solution, your brand, or price. You are the number one influence.
2. You have far more control and influence than you may realize. How you sell matters more than anything else.
3. This can work for you or against you.

For these reasons, it is critical that you deliver a valuable and enjoyable experience in every encounter.

Training Your Client

By consistently delivering value, we train our prospects to see us as valuable assets, domain experts, trusted advisors, and precious resources who can help them achieve the outcomes they desire.

When buyers see you in this way:

- They will share more information with you.
- They will ask for advice and accept your recommendations.
- They will refer you to others.
- They will forgive your mistakes.
- They will protect and warn you.
- You will increase your sales both in number and dollar volume.

According to Cahners, trusted advisors are 69% more likely to come away with the sale.

The two keys to becoming a trusted advisor:
1. Value - Delivering what the client considers to be of genuine value
2. Consistency - Delivering that value in every experience with the client

EXERCISE #26 - Extrapolation Bias - Part 1

Instructions: Using the illustration below (and without looking ahead) plot the next point or two on the chart below. What do you think will happen next?

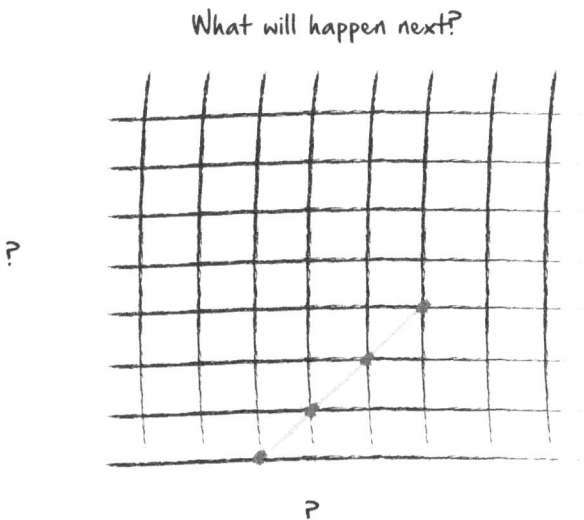

Extrapolation Bias

When you consider all the details of a product or service, most buyers spend a surprisingly small amount of time evaluating choices. They realize they can never fully assess every aspect of the solution, so they rely on trust, rapport, and good intent. This is especially true for complex solutions where trust and external validation weigh heavily.

Have you ever lost a sale to a competitor whose offering was clearly inferior?

The time a prospect spends with a salesperson before the sale is an indicator of their experience after the sale. Each interaction with you is a "sample." Prospects are sampling their experience with you as much as they are evaluating the product or deliverable. In many cases (with service offerings especially) the experience during the sale is weighted far above the product itself or the methodology used.

This experience sample, because it is relatively small, makes clients prone to a cognitive bias known as extrapolation bias – a form of availability bias where we overestimate probabilities of events associated with memorable or dramatic occurrences.

With extrapolation bias we extrapolate the outcome of future events based on a narrow sampling of current events. For example, if a stock is going up we may extrapolate that it will continue to go up. Or, if our experience at a restaurant is good, we extrapolate that it will always be good.

 # EXERCISE #26 - Extrapolation Bias - Part 2

Instructions: Look back to your plotting on the chart in Part 1 of this exercise. With the limited information you were given at that time, did you forecast that the trend would continue on its previous trajectory? Had you been given the full picture below, might you have forecasted differently?

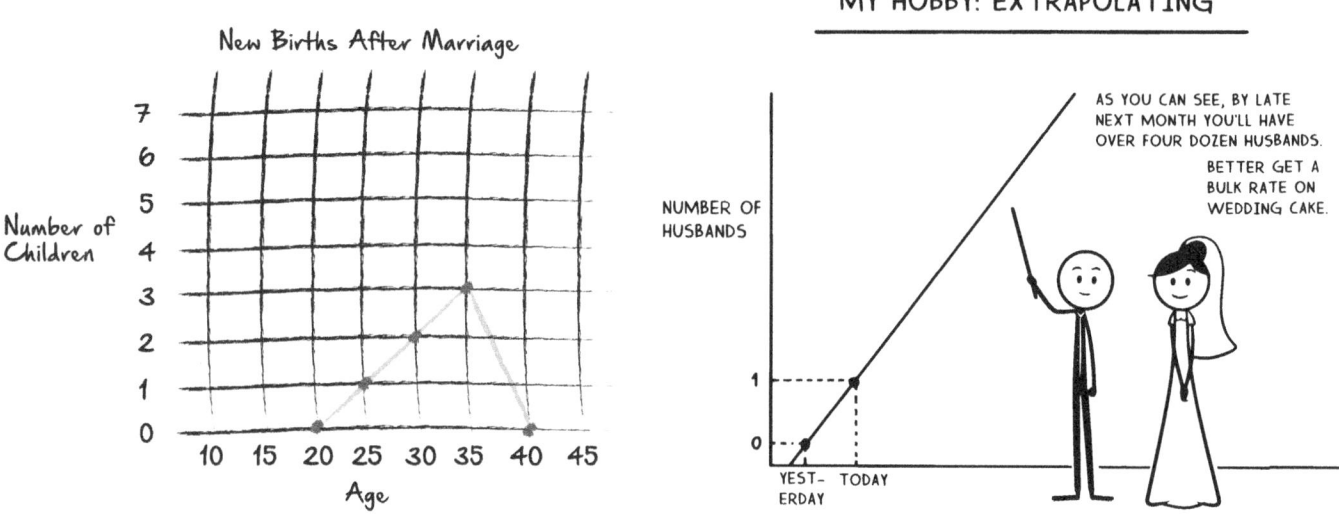

Group Discussion: What is the problem with the cartoon above? How does that relate to our sales encounters with clients?

With this backdrop it is easy to see the importance of each sales experience sample. In general, prospects will take the sum of their experiences with us and extrapolate them into what they think all future experiences will be. This can work for you or against you.

> ## Prospects will take the sum of their experiences with us and extrapolate them into what they think all future experiences will be.

How did you lose to a competitor that was clearly inferior? Your prospect's narrow sampling from your competitor may have been exceptional while their sampling of you may have been sub-par. This is especially true with complex solutions because prospects can never really get a sample adequate enough to fully understand all the dimensions of each offering – so, they extrapolate and come to the wrong conclusion.

 CLOSING SECRET - How you sell is a sample of how you solve.

So, how did you lose to a clearly inferior solution? You were outsold.

In selling we often hear that phrase, but now, rather than taking it as a mindless quip or insult, you'll understand some of the mechanics involved.

When Clients Go Silent

Sellers commonly complain when a prospect stops responding. While there are many reasons for this, by far the greatest is that the salesperson has not been adding enough value throughout the process, and the prospect has concluded the salesperson has nothing worthwhile to offer.

Often, their communication mysteriously stops after they receive the proposal. This is especially true for buyers who are price driven. Having received what they perceive to be the last useful piece of information – the price – they cease communicating because they have no further use for us.

Remedy this problem by providing value beyond data and information on every encounter. If there is a problem with your proposal or the price, they will share that with you and provide the feedback you need to correct it. Teach them to value their time with you, and they will call upon you for the valuable insights you possess long past the close of the sale.

By training them to see you as a trusted advisor, prospects will buy, and clients will return to you again and again.

Clients Have Redefined Value

Revenue Storm recently surveyed B2B and B2C companies and pitted these two sets of values against each other to determine which set clients valued more:

- **Value Category 1**
    - Ability to fulfill an order or request
    - Ability to provide the best offering or price
    - Ability to respond and listen when approached
- **Value Category 2**
    - Ability to challenge current thinking
    - Ability to proactively bring innovative ideas
    - Ability to provide thought leadership

82% of respondents valued the items in Category 2 more than the items in Category 1.

This reveals that elements like fulfillment, overall value, and responsiveness are important and will always be part of the value equation, however, they have become expected – a minimum requirement to even get in the game. The ability to deliver insight and thought leadership are critical to buyers when selecting a business partner.

What Customers Value Most

We know the buyer's ability to instantly research and compare solutions via the Internet is rapidly commoditizing most industries. This means sellers who are unable to add value to the sales experience won't have much to differentiate with beyond price.

Fortunately, research by Huthwaite reveals that buyers are willing to pay a premium under the following circumstances:
- The seller identified an Unanticipated Solution for the buyer's problems.
- The seller identified an Unrecognized Problem the buyer was experiencing.
- The seller identified an Unseen Opportunity.
- The seller acted as more than just a vendor of products and services but instead as a Broker of Strengths (their term).

Take a look at the first three circumstances in this list. They all point to something that is new and unexpected to the buyer. This important observation helps us understand the key to delivering what customers want most – insight.

Buyers will forgo price concerns when additional value is delivered by the sales process itself.

I call this unanticipated value that a client or prospect receives as a result of our meeting "Unexpected Value."

If we want to maximize value, we need to inject some unexpected value into every sales encounter, and it needs to come as a bit of a surprise.

The Top 7 Methods to Add Value to Every Sales Encounter
1. Deliver Insight
2. Employ Powerful Questions
3. Help Them Better Understand Their Needs
4. Help Them See the Path to Success
5. Share New Ideas
6. Deliver Education
7. Share News, Trigger Events, & Trends from Their Industry

These are listed in descending order for effectiveness, so delivering insight is more valuable to clients than delivering news. But, they can all add value to your meetings.

#1 – Delivering Insight

Of all the aspects customers value – they value new, relevant insights the most. They want insight, help, and guidance beyond a basic understanding of their challenges. To deliver that, you must go beyond the data dump of product and service knowledge.

The key point here is: Data is not insight.

> Data is not insight.

Let me illustrate with a personal story.

My youngest son Justin began having health issues at the age of eight while attending third grade. He was experiencing intermittent stomach pains and bouts of diarrhea. For months we tried all the standard remedies to no avail. We took him to physicians who employed their own series of treatments, also with no success.

During this period Justin developed an even worse symptom – severe depression. Every day, at home or at school, became emotionally taxing not only for him but also for those around him. I will be candid and confess that as a loving parent it was the most challenging experience I have ever encountered. Sadness and frustration do not begin to describe my feelings. Each day promised him a combination of physical pain, diarrhea, and emotional trial – and I was powerless to stop it. Often, I wished I could take his ailments upon myself so that he could experience relief.

Unfortunately, this continued for two years until Justin was finally diagnosed with Crohn's disease. By this time, however, it had become life-threatening. Justin was chronically dehydrated and anemic. He developed dark circles around his eyes, and the smallest exertion would completely deplete his energy. His skin became pale and yellow, and he developed sores around his mouth that refused to heal. He also developed insomnia, so he literally could get no respite from his condition. He would crawl into bed with my wife and me, and we would try our best to comfort him.

But, at least, finally, we had something – we had a solid diagnosis. Initially, I knew nothing of Crohn's disease, but with a desire to save my son's life I dove headlong into research and turned up thousands of pages of contradictory data on Crohn's disease. It was overwhelming. But, it was my job, as Justin's loving father, to turn data into something valuable – information and insight.

In desperation I reviewed tremendous amounts of data. I organized the data and slowly distilled it into a coherent picture (what I would call information). I felt I understood Crohn's – what it was and how it worked. I had usable information now, but I was still missing something. I needed a clear path of what to do with my newfound knowledge. I needed insight.

Prospects and clients need the same. They have access to data. They have access to information. There was a time when clients valued data and information, but that day is gone. What clients want is insight. They want help understanding and designing a clear path that will lead them to their desired outcome. Just as I sought, clients want the actionable steps that understanding the information provides.

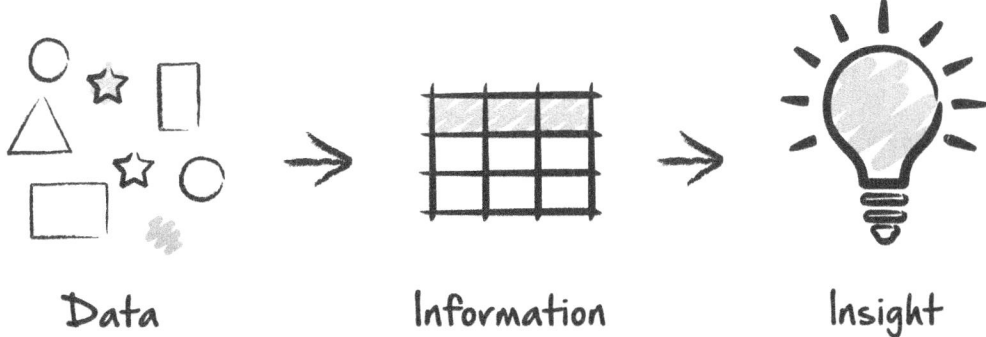

Ultimately, I identified a few individuals who shared with me practical insights on how we might treat Justin's condition in a non-steroidal, non-surgical way. Within a few months of administering this regimen, Justin recovered and remains in complete remission.

I have tremendous respect and gratitude for these pioneering practitioners who helped me heal my son. I share this story with you because these are the same emotions – respect and gratitude – that you engender in your clients when you provide them with genuinely valuable insights.

We add value to clients by saving time for them by synthesizing information into actionable insight.

What Makes Good Insight?

Three criteria make insight valuable:

1. It must be relevant.
2. It must be novel.
3. It must be actionable.

Relevant - Relevance is both subjective and contextual. It is subjective because what is relevant to one person may not be relevant to another – one person's signal is another person's noise. Relevance is also contextual since what proves to be a valuable insight affecting the business as a whole may not be very valuable to the janitor who is not greatly affected by it.

It doesn't matter how valuable you feel your insight is. It only matters whether the person you're talking to finds it relevant in their current context. Your prospect is the judge – not you.

Novel - The insight you share must provide something new – something not already known. Again, this is subjective. What you know may be very different from what your prospect knows. New information to you may be old information to them. As the Huthwaite study proves, clients find new insights regarding problems, solutions, and opportunities very valuable. So much so, that they are willing to pay a premium for the solutions related to them.

Actionable - The insight you share must be actionable – something they can do something about. If it doesn't suggest an action they can take, your client won't find it useful. Ideally, the insight you share will suggest something actionable that relates to the solution you provide.

The basic formula for what makes good insight is:

$$\text{Relevant} + \text{Novel} + \text{Actionable} = \text{Good Insight}$$

What Kind of Insight? The Key to Adding Value is Preparation

Being thoughtful and deliberate in your planning before each meeting is the key to adding value on every encounter. Do not try to add value on-the-fly. That's winging it, and professionals do not wing it.

In an upcoming chapter we will introduce you to forms that you can use to help you prepare, but a good old piece of paper and pencil can do the job just as well. This process also complements many of the sales methodologies you might already be using.

Know What Stage of the Buying Process Your Prospect is In

Buyers go through eight distinctive stages whenever making a purchase.

1. Unaware
2. Awareness
3. Define Problem
4. Consider Options
5. Evaluate Solutions
6. Justify Decision
7. Final Selection
8. Implementation

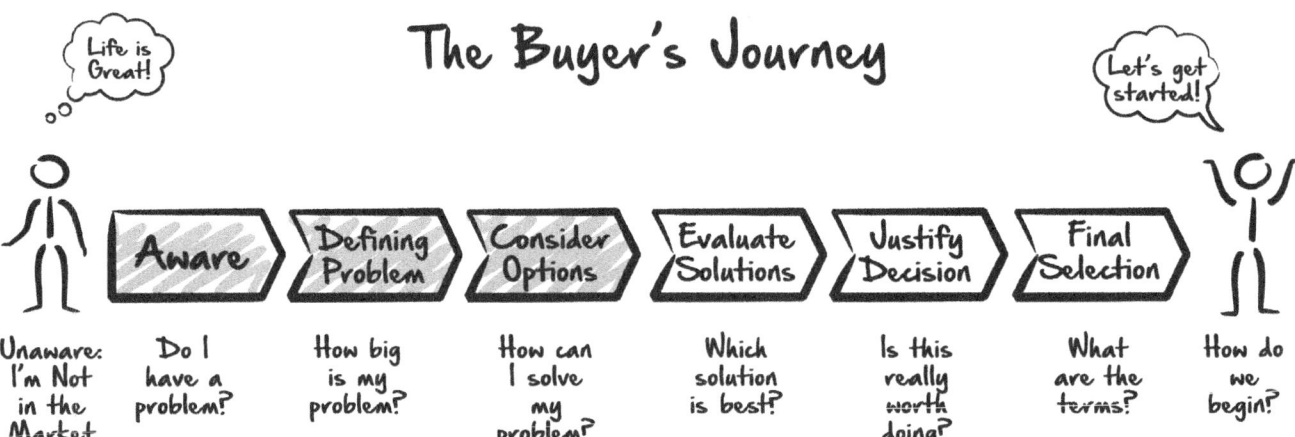

Buyers ask and gather answers distinctive to each stage. Knowing what stage your prospect is in prepares you to maximize the value you bring. Consider the context of where your prospect is in the buying process. For example:

- If they are still only grasping that there is a need for change, then you might offer insight as to the gap between where they are and where they could be or should be.
- If they are aware of certain challenges but those problems are not crystallized in their minds, you might help them quantify the potential impact of their current problems or the upside that could be attained with a particular solution.
- If they have quantified the upside potential, you might help them identify various options or tradeoffs to consider in order to achieve their desired outcome.
- If they are considering a few specific solutions, you might help them understand which are best matched to their desired results.
- If they have identified a particular path to achieve their goals, you might help them outline the plan or steps they need to take to reach their goal.
- If they are settled on a particular approach or solution, you might alert them to pitfalls to avoid and suggest ways to reduce risks associated with moving forward.
- If they are at the stage of finalizing their decision, you might share strategies to get executive approval and advise them on the most beneficial business model or terms.
- If they are preparing to implement a given solution or approach, you might recommend ways to leverage their new capabilities once the new solution is employed, and how to take their game to the next logical step.

There are infinite ways to add value at any stage of the buying cycle. The point is to be cognizant of where your prospect is, so you can offer the kind of value they will consider the most important at that stage. It would be inappropriate or unwise to suggest a specific set of steps to implement a solution when your prospect hasn't yet quantified their challenge and determined whether it's worth addressing.

> Be cognizant of where your prospect is in buying process, so you can offer the kind of value they will consider the most important at that stage.

To guide your thinking as you plan each encounter, ask yourself, "What stage of the buying cycle is my prospect/client in?" Then ask, "What would they consider most valuable at this stage?"

Developing Insights

Delivering insight is the primary way you add value to each client encounter. To get you started developing your own valuable insights for your particular market and solutions, I offer the following outline of steps:

- ✓ Understand and prioritize your prospect's ultimate goals and primary concerns.
- ✓ Identify the key business and industry drivers and sub-drivers behind those goals and concerns. We want to know what drives them to invest or take action.
- ✓ Map the relationships between these goals, concerns, drivers and sub-drivers to understand their cause and effect.
- ✓ Detail your own offering's key strengths and differentiators with respect to the drivers.
- ✓ Test assumptions regarding your insight. Start with sales to refine your insight before testing it with prospect surveys or by speaking with customers.

- ✓ Explore where you can inject intervention points to create new value or achieve a better result. Here are 3 good places to consider:
  - Reveal a new or unidentified driver or need.
  - Change the impact of a driver or demonstrate that its effect is different than imagined.
  - Uncover a previously unknown connection between drivers that affect results.
- ✓ Develop a compelling story line, supported by data, to give prospects cause to question their current perspective and thinking.
- ✓ Develop a messaging plan around your new viable and unique insight. Messaging should be focused to disrupt prospect thinking, so that their purchase criteria are reset and they become open to alternative solutions.

#2 – Prepare Powerful Questions

Your questions, in and of themselves, have an amazing capacity to create insight and bring value. Questions that do not produce value are a waste of time. Your ability to master questioning and facilitative dialogue is among the highest payoff skills. The key to a valuable question is that the answer provokes change for the better. When we ask questions that facilitate new understanding – how a prospect can improve their condition – they are deemed valuable.

The Buyer's

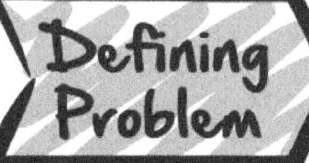

Unaware Not in the Market	Do I have a problem?	How big is my problem?	How can I solve my problem?
Value Strategies	**Value Strategies**	**Value Strategies**	**Value Strategies**
Offer: Insight on the gap between where they are & where they could/should be. Create awareness. Identify industry challenges.	Offer: Measurement criteria & metrics. Impact assessment tools. Comparisons to other issues & challenges. Problem ROI / business cases.	Help quantify the potential impact of current problems and/or upside with a given opportunity.	Help them understand which options are best matched to their desired results. Offer comparisons of alternative solution methods & "How to solve" articles.

Journey

Let's get started!

Evaluate Solutions → **Justify decision** → **Final Selection**

Evaluate Solutions	Justify decision	Final Selection	
Which solution is best?	Is this really worth doing?	What are the terms?	How do we begin?
Value Strategies	**Value Strategies**	**Value Strategies**	**Value Strategies**
Alert them to pitfalls. Suggest ways to reduce risks associated with moving forward. Vendor comparisons. Industry rankings / reports. Reference accounts.	Offer: Business case / ROI tools. Project Plans. Case studies. Reference accounts. Proposals.	Advise them on the most beneficial business model or terms. Share consensus & executive approval strategies.	Offer best practice advice. Project Plans. Recommend ways to leverage their new capabilities & take their game to the next logical step.

EXERCISE #27 - Powerful Questions - Part 1

Instructions: Write out the questions you typically ask during your sales encounters in the first column below. We'll return later to complete the other columns.

Question	Benefits?	Knowledge	Cognitive	Prompts Higher Level Thinking

Unfortunately, the most common questions are simply requests for information which do nothing to facilitate new understanding for the customer. While we must ask basic information-gathering questions from time to time, it is important to remember that prospects get no benefit from them. Since the prospect already knows the answer, the value is all one-sided – yours. Often, the answers to basic questions are found in the company's marketing collateral or website. Research in advance.

True value-adding questions are those to which the client does not already know the answer or has not even thought of. They require thought, encourage reflection, advance the conversation into new territory, and the eventual answers add value to the individuals involved.

True value-adding questions are those to which the client does not already know the answer.

Stimulate Your Buyer's Thinking

There are two dimensions along which your questions stimulate thinking:

1. Knowledge
2. Cognitive

Knowledge Dimension

Factual	Conceptual	Procedural	Metacognitive
Knowledge of terminology Knowledge of specific details & elements	Knowledge of classifications & categories Knowledge of principles & generalizations Knowledge of theories, models & structures	Knowledge of subject-specific skills & algorithms Knowledge of subject-specific techniques & methods Knowledge of criteria for determining when to use appropriate procedures	Strategic knowledge Knowledge about cognitive tasks, including appropriate contextual & conditional knowledge Self-knowledge

Concrete knowledge ⟵──────────────⟶ Abstract knowledge

Knowledge - Questions stimulate awareness along the knowledge dimension which spans from simple facts, to concepts, to processes, and then an awareness of their own knowledge of a given area.

To share knowledge, it is important that you have some. How would you rate yourself on a scale of 1-10 in the subject area you are trying to sell? Commit yourself to becoming an expert in your field so you have a broad range of knowledge to draw upon when crafting your questions and facilitating understanding.

Cognitive Dimension

Remember	Understand	Apply	Analyze	Evaluate	Create
Identifying Recalling	Interpreting, clarifying, translating Illustrating, exemplifying Categorizing, classifying Summarizing, generalizing, abstracting Concluding, predicting, extrapolating, inferring Comparing, contrasting, matching Explaining, constructing models	Executing, carrying out Implementing, using	Differentiating, discriminating, distinguishing, focusing, selecting Organizing, finding coherence, integrating, parsing, structuring Attributing, deconstructing	Checking, coordinating, detecting, monitoring, testing Critiquing, judging	Generating, hypothesizing Planning, designing Producing, constructing

Lower order thinking ⟵————————————⟶ Higher order thinking

Cognitive - Questions stimulate increasingly complex thinking along the cognitive dimension which spans from basic recall, to understanding, to applying the concept to themselves, to clearly analyzing and organizing the concept, to evaluating, differentiating, judging, and finally to creating their own designs based on the concept.

The further your questions are along these spectrums, the more value your buyer will perceive from your questions. For example, along the knowledge spectrum, clients will not value questions that require them to rattle off a list of business facts as much as questions that require them to consider the steps they will take to achieve an outcome and where they are currently in that process. Along the cognitive spectrum, buyers do not value questions that cause them to simply recall or understand concepts as much as they value questions that cause them to reflect, evaluate, and judge the details in a given area.

Unfortunately, the vast majority of questions in sales interactions are simply about facts and understanding – both along the lower end of the spectrums of these dimensions. That is not to say that facts and understanding are not important, they are. It's simply that those questions are not highly valued by prospects.

EXERCISE #27 - Powerful Questions - Part 2

Instructions: Refer back to Part 1 of this exercise on page 84, and for each question that you typically ask, complete the remaining columns as outlined below.

Benefits? - Write who this question benefits (Me, Customer, or Both).

Knowledge - Where on the knowledge spectrum does your question belong? Factual, Conceptual, Procedural, or Metacognitive (see diagram for reference).

Cognitive - where on the cognitive spectrum does your question belong? Remember, Understand, Apply, Analyze, Evaluate, or Create (see diagram for reference).

Prompts Higher Level Thinking - write Yes or No if this question prompts higher-level thinking.

 Group Discussion: Break into groups of 3 or 4 and review your questions and results. Did any patterns emerge? Share what you discovered with the entire group.

EXERCISE #27 - Powerful Questions - Part 3

Instructions: Review the sample questions below and complete the columns using the same criteria as in Part 2.

Question	Benefits?	Knowledge	Cognitive	Prompts Higher Level Thinking
What drivers would you say are most affecting your interest in addressing your challenge or opportunity?				
What sort of impact would a solution have on each of your key stakeholders?				
During your evaluation, what are the steps you will be going through as a company?				
As you do your evaluation what process will you be using to include and garner feedback and consensus from all stakeholders?				
As you evaluate and design your solution how will you go about ensuring that the solution ultimately meets everyone's needs?				
As you assemble your evaluation team, how will you determine which priorities will be most heavily weighted?				
As you design what you feel will be the ideal solution, what criteria will you use to evaluate options?				
As you reflect on possible trade-offs or compromises, how will you determine which elements will be the most important?				
As you reflect on your progress thus far, what do you anticipate will be the biggest challenges to integrating this into your current environment?				

Group Discussion: Discuss your answers and observations a group.

EXERCISE #27 - Powerful Questions - Part 4

Instructions: Using what you've learned, create some high-value questions for your type of sale.

Then, if possible, break into groups of 3 or 4 to evaluate each other's questions and complete the criteria under each category. Within your group, select the two best examples and write them on a flipchart or whiteboard.

Note: High-value questions are contextual in their value. It is not always best to ask questions that are highest on each spectrum. Use the context of where your customer is in their process to develop and select your high-value questions.

Question	Benefits?	Knowledge	Cognitive	Prompts Higher Level Thinking

Group Discussion: Share your examples and what was learned with the entire group.

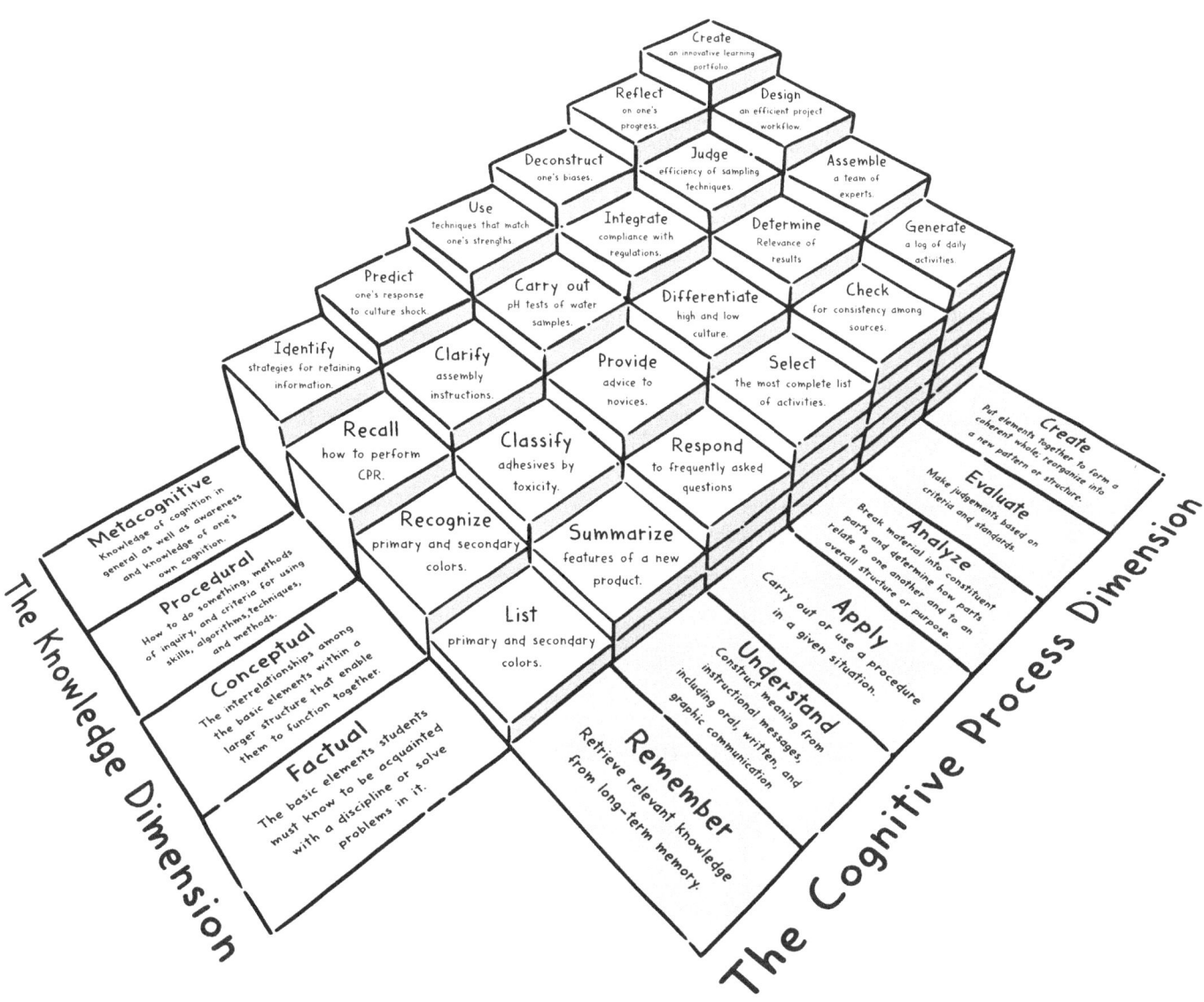

Combining Dimensions

When we prompt higher-level thinking, we add value. Asking tough, powerful questions define you as a consultant and communicate your intent to genuinely help. This alone will add a great deal of value to each encounter and differentiate you from competitors.

EXERCISE #28 - The Dynamics of High-Value Questions

Instructions: Complete the assessment below, and use the following Score Key to tally your scores.

	Rarely				Frequently
I find silence after my question awkward.	1	2	3	4	5
I rephrase my questions frequently.	1	2	3	4	5
I ask a new question before they've answered my original question because I think I should have asked something else.	1	2	3	4	5
I frequently make an additional comment or clarification after my questions.	1	2	3	4	5
I find myself frequently answering my own questions.	1	2	3	4	5
I wait less than a second or two before making a follow-up question or comment.	1	2	3	4	5
Responses from my customer seem agonizingly slow.	1	2	3	4	5
I fill up silence with talking or commentary.	1	2	3	4	5
I immediately comment or sell after my customer responds.	1	2	3	4	5
I frequently ask multiple questions at once.	1	2	3	4	5
Total Score:	< ---- Total Row				

Score Key

10-15	Excellent	You have zen-like patience.
16-25	Good	You are in the top 15% of sales professionals in this area.
26-35	Fair	Your results will be unpredictable. Consider areas of improvement.
36-45	Poor	Learning opportunity. You have significant room for improvement.
46-50	Very Poor	Your questioning skills are sabotaging your results.

Group Discussion: Break into groups of 3-4 and discuss your responses and any patterns or insights discovered. Share the top two with the entire group.

Dynamics of High-Value Questions

Higher-level questions force clients to think in ways they haven't before. Their "Aha" moment is the source of the value in the question. Often, they will have to synthesize the new thinking right on the spot. You can actually see it happening. Because of this, be aware of these dynamics:

- Wait for them to respond. Studies show that salespeople only wait about one second before either rephrasing their question, asking a new question, making an additional comment, or even trying to answer the question for the client. The urge to fill the silence is uncontrollable. Resist.

  Give clients time to reflect and synthesize their answer. Wait at least three or four seconds before speaking, so they can contemplate what you have asked them and formulate an answer.

  After their initial answer, wait at least another three or four seconds because often the client is thinking out loud, and they will augment their answer shortly after their reply – but only if you stay quiet and allow them to finish their thoughts. In group situations another person might jump in to add information or detail. You want this. Patience at these two intervals, elicits two to five times more information from buyers. More importantly, clients value their experience far greater.

  It takes amazing self-control to pause while clients cognate. Use this tip to make waiting easy: Take notes. Show that you are preparing to take notes as you ask your question. As they respond begin writing their comments, you will automatically get the four seconds of silence you need to prompt more information. After their reply, continue writing through the silence as that prompts them to provide more and more information during your silent note taking. It's quite remarkable.

- Because high-level questions require more thought or mental "CPU cycles," it is important to use them judiciously. Be selective about what you ask. Two or three questions per encounter is probably ideal, though my personal experience is that five is the upper limit before they start to perceive your questions negatively.

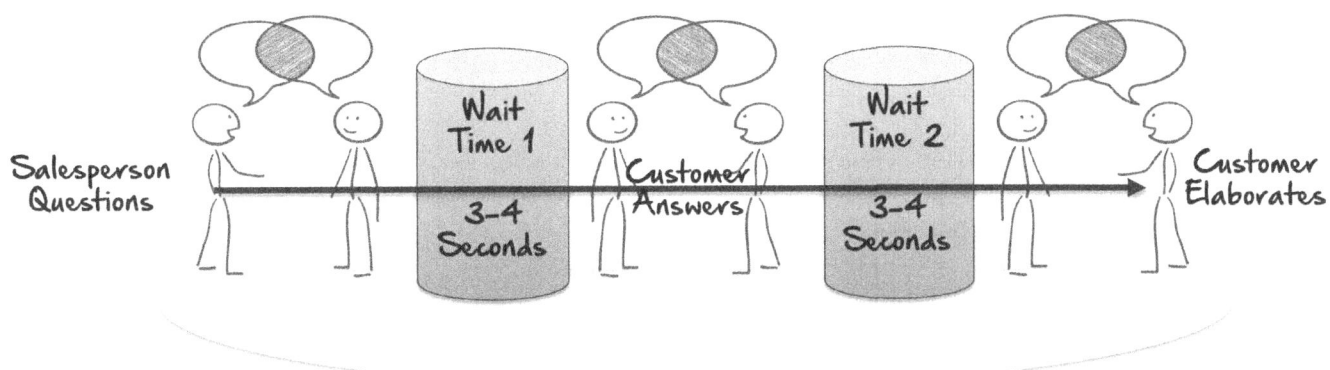

A few examples of high-value questions:

- As you assemble your evaluation team, how will you determine which priorities will be most heavily weighted?
- As you design what you feel will be the ideal solution, what criteria will you use to evaluate options?
- As you reflect on possible trade-offs or compromises, how will you determine which elements will be the most important?
- During your evaluation, what are the steps you will be going through as a company?
- As you reflect on your progress thus far, what do you anticipate will be the biggest challenges to integrating this into your current environment?

Many experts consider questions your most valuable tool. The right questions are facilitative and help both you and the buyer uncover what they value most. They uncover the hierarchy of individual preferences and preferred outcomes. They reveal personal agendas and the influence dynamics between those involved in the decision.

In addition to adding value, the right questions will:

- Engage your clients
- Direct their attention to the topics most important for them to consider
- Facilitate new connections in their minds and help them synthesize new understanding
- Assist clients in discovering their own answers
- Facilitate learning through articulation
- Enhance memory
- Elicit feedback
- Clarify issues and eliminate assumptions
- Increase confidence

Most importantly, the right questions are perceived as valuable. They build rapport and trust, establish you as a consultant, and prove that you and the client are aligned in your interests. Because high-value questions require planning before each meeting, they differentiate you from competitors in a very big way. Repeating this experience with clients and prospects during each encounter trains them to see you as a trusted advisor which keeps you close to them during and after the sale.

> *High-value questions require planning before each meeting.*

To explore this subject further, I highly recommend Deb Calvert's book *DISCOVER Questions Get You Connected: for professional sellers*. I agree with her statement, "There is no easier and more affordable way to create genuine, personalized value for each and every buyer."

#3 – Help Clients Better Understand Their Needs

One outcome of superior questions is clients come to better understand their own needs. When you assist them in understanding and objectifying their needs (and as a result the requirements to meet those needs) you are adding value.

Performing an excellent discovery with the prospect will facilitate mutual understanding of what it will take for them to succeed. Your discovery can also help them better understand their own internal dynamics and give them a firm grasp of the tools needed to move their organization forward.

Professional discovery skills are essential. Prospects will always value a professionally executed discovery.

#4 – Help Clients See the Path to Success

When considering a new project, idea, or solution customers are unsure about how its adoption will affect their organization. The path to success is cloudy. When the steps ahead are unclear, they perceive heightened risk, and they slow down or even halt their progress as they assess all the dynamics associated with moving forward.

With complex projects, they may embark on a project like this only once in a lifetime. Sellers in this category are perfectly positioned to add value because your experiences (tips, stories, planning tools, sample project plans, outcomes of similar clients, etc.) represent tremendous value. Help them set clear steps that lead to success. In some cases, the value you bring can surpass the value of the solution itself and positions you as a consultant and trusted advisor. Leverage this unexpected value in every opportunity.

Present a clear vision of how to achieve their objectives, or help them develop their own vision, and you are adding value.

> *Present a clear vision of how your prospect can achieve their objectives, or help them develop their own vision, and you are adding value.*

You will find recommended reading at the end of this workbook that can aid you in leveraging your experience to help clients see the path to success.

#5 – Share New Ideas

Ron Baker, founder of VeraSage Institute and author of *Mind Over Matter*, says, "Ideas have always and everywhere been more valuable than the physical act of carrying them out. In the arena of business, ideas have an enormous capacity to apply knowledge to knowledge, thereby increasing innovation and wealth."

Not every idea you bring will be weighed equally from your prospect's perspective. However, there is value inherent in your ideas regardless of whether your prospect employs them. Offer all the valuable ideas you can.

Your experiences in implementing your products and services will likely far outweigh your prospect's experience. So, thoughts and ideas in this area will be seen as helpful. Share how your other clients have:

- Reduced costs
- Increased revenues
- Garnered additional business
- Saved time
- Managed resources
- Improved a process
- Improved quality/outcomes
- Simplified tasks
- Solved a particular problem/challenge
- Successfully implemented something
- Made their job easier
- Used their existing solution in a new way
- Utilized a service that they had overlooked

These are like "best practices" for your clients. Take time to identify which of these your prospects would find most valuable and build on it, tailoring them to your prospect's situation to maximize their perception of value.

#6 – Deliver Education

Insight derives from education. Become a diligent student of your industry's best practices. Consider developing educational sessions either occasionally or on a regular basis. The cost is usually minimal, yet the customer's perception of value can be huge. When possible, collect feedback from attendees and use these examples as valuable adjuncts to share in future educational sessions.

Educate clients and prospects every time you encounter them, and they will value and anticipate every interaction with you. Further, they will be eager to brag about their new resource (you) with colleagues and that will develop new relationships and opportunities.

#7 – Share News, Trigger Events, and Insights from Their Industry

Sharing news, trigger events, and insights from their industry can add value so long as your prospects are not already aware of them. Remember, it must be new and unexpected. By and large, this falls towards the weaker end of the spectrum when it comes to adding value, but if it's actually news to them and relevant, it will be seen as valuable.

> *In some cases, the value you bring in these areas can surpass the value of the solution itself and will position you as a consultant and trusted advisor.*

EXERCISE #29 - Adding Value to Each Encounter - Brainstorm

Instructions: Brainstorm ideas for each of the remaining five methods for adding value. Review the Priming Questions for each method below, then on the following page write your ideas for implementing these value-adding elements to your sales encounters.

Priming Questions

Help Them Better Understand Their Needs

- What tells the customer that they have a challenge or need?
- How is that challenge or need measured? What are the metrics?
    - What are these values now? What are the industry averages?
    - What do they want them to be or what is a good goal or objective? What's possible?
    - What is the value of the difference?
    - What is that value over time?
- What have they already tried to address this challenge? What have others in the industry tried?
    - What are the challenges with those approaches? Why didn't they work?
    - What does that reveal about their true needs?

Help Them See the Path to Success

- Who else has accomplished your customers goal or objective?
- What steps did they take to get there?
- What steps will help the customer see how they can achieve their success?
- What does the project plan to achieve success look like?
- What resources will be required for success?

Share New Ideas

- What sources can you leverage from your customers and industry?
- What concepts or ideas are new to your customer or industry?
- What is the potential of leveraging these ideas?
- What are the challenges?

Deliver Education

- What education topics would your customer find valuable?
- What channels are best for delivering this education?
- What resources will you need to deliver this education?

Share News, Trigger Events & Insights from Their Industry

- What sources can you leverage for news, trigger events and insight about your customers industry?
- Which news, insights or trigger events are they not likely to know?
- What is the best way to incorporate these into your encounters?

Adding Value to Each Encounter – Brainstorm

☑ Help them better understand their needs.
   ☑ Help them see the path to success.
      ☑ Share new ideas.
         ☑ Deliver education.
            ☑ Share news, trigger events & insights from their industry.

- Value to Customer – why this idea is of value to your customer?
- Client Action Items – what actionable steps does this idea suggest for your client?
- Action Items for Me – what might you need to do to implement this idea?
- Sales Asset? – does this idea suggest the creation of a new sales asset? If so, detail.
- Priority – prioritize so you can focus on the highest impact ideas first.

❑ ❑ ❑ ❑ ❑ Idea: _____ Priority: _____

Value to customer: _____

Client action items: _____

Actions items for me: _____

Sales asset? _____

❑ ❑ ❑ ❑ ❑ Idea: _____ Priority: _____

Value to customer: _____

Client action items: _____

Actions items for me: _____

Sales asset? _____

❑ ❑ ❑ ❑ ❑ Idea: _____ Priority: _____

Value to customer: _____

Client action items: _____

Actions items for me: _____

Sales asset? _____

❑ ❑ ❑ ❑ ❑ Idea: _____ Priority: _____

Value to customer: _____

Client action items: _____

Actions items for me: _____

Sales asset? _____

❏ ❏ ❏ ❏ ❏ Idea: _____ Priority: _____

Value to customer: _____

Client action items: _____

Actions items for me: _____

Sales asset? _____

❏ ❏ ❏ ❏ ❏ Idea: _____ Priority: _____

Value to customer: _____

Client action items: _____

Actions items for me: _____

Sales asset? _____

Group Discussion: Break into groups of 3-4 and share ideas. What new ideas can you add to each area? Write your top ideas on a flipchart or whiteboard. Each group now shares their top ideas with the entire group. All ideas are now cataloged by someone in the group as a resource for everyone.

Become a Domain Expert

To consistently provide insight, innovative thinking, and unanticipated solutions put forth the effort to become a top expert in your domain. Where your expertise and facilitation intersect, your clients will find great value, and you will find great success.

Additional Resources

Further explore how to add value to your sales encounters at PureMuir.com/TPCworkbook and find more creative ideas on this topic.

🔑 **CLOSING SECRET** - The key to adding value is preparation.

Conclusion

"How can I provide value on this encounter?" is almost universally ignored in selling today. If you can't articulate what the prospect will gain from your meeting, the meeting will be a waste of time (not the kind of sample we want to deliver).

How we sell is a sample of how we solve, and prospects are sampling our value on every encounter. They sum up their experiences with us and extrapolate what their future experiences with us (and the solutions we represent) will be – which can work for or against us.

By consistently delivering Unexpected Value on every encounter we train prospects and clients to see us as valuable resources, domain experts, and trusted advisors who can help them achieve the outcomes they desire. Fortunately, the number of ways to do this is limitless. The key is to prepare. Professionals do not wing it.

In the next chapter, we'll learn how to plan each encounter so it's maximally valuable and productive.

CHAPTER 11

Planning Sales Encounters

"Planning maximizes the value of the call to the customer."

– David Brock

You are now fully equipped to plan and execute a high-value meeting with your prospective client. Being a professional means planning. Productivity and success don't happen by accident. It is the result of planning, commitment, and focused effort. There are two strategic types of benefits to planning – tactical and contemplative.

Tactical - Planning is beneficial from a tactical perspective because it results in the actual words you will say, questions you will ask, and areas you will address. Knowing these in advance will greatly improve your confidence and your effectiveness. It will also produce an agenda (see below) which will give you and your prospect awareness in where you are and the sequence you will follow during the course of your meeting.

Contemplative - Planning is beneficial from a contemplative perspective because it forces us to slow down and think in ways we wouldn't have otherwise. It allows us to contemplate what we don't know and reminds us to consider important dynamics that could have been overlooked.

As sellers we tend to be action-oriented. We favor jumping right in to make something happen. For many, planning is unfamiliar or even uncomfortable territory. One of the marks of a true professional is working smart in addition to working hard.

In this chapter we will make planning quick and efficient for you by distilling all you have learned thus far into a set of easy-to-follow steps.

First, a brief review...

7 Primary Reasons to Plan Every Sales Encounter:
1. You will be far more effective - We learned earlier that sales planning is strongly correlated with success. Neil Rackham declared through research that, "Good selling depends on good planning more than any other single factor."
2. It increases the probability you will achieve your intended outcome - The old expression, "Failing to plan is planning to fail," is still true today. Knowing in advance what you want to achieve significantly increases your odds of achieving it.
3. It will help you remember the questions you want to ask - Strong value-add questions are hard to create on the fly. Planning in advance will allow you to craft excellent questions and remind you to ask them in the heat of the moment.
4. It creates a checklist of steps to follow - Planning gives you a roadmap to gaining the contacts, information, and commitments you need for a successful outcome.
5. It gives you time to prepare your Unexpected Value - Considering what unexpected value is best for your prospect during your upcoming encounter depends on where your prospect is in their buying cycle. Planning gives you the time to maximize your value.
6. It increases the probability you will achieve your prospect's intended outcome - You only succeed when they succeed. Consistently planning ensures they will achieve what they expect – from this meeting as well as the entire sale.

7. It differentiates you from the competition - Few salespeople give much thought to planning their sales encounters in terms of the value their prospect will receive, so planning a cohesive and valuable meeting alone will differentiate you from your competition.

CLOSING SECRET - Productivity and success don't happen by accident. You and your meetings will be more productive when you plan.

In previous chapters we:

- Got our mindset right
- Defined our sales objective
- Defined our call objective
- Reviewed our value proposition
- Brainstormed our possible advances, and
- Created ways to provide unexpected value

If you have completed all exercises in the previous chapters, planning your sales encounter will be very straightforward. Forms in this workbook and at PureMuir.com/TPCworkbook can help with this process, but all you really need is a simple piece of paper and a pen. It is also compatible and complementary with today's major sales methodologies. So, this will dovetail nicely into your current process. And, over time this will go very quickly.

The Six Elements of Sales Encounter Planning

Regardless of the methodology or tools you use to plan each sales encounter, you should cover these six elements:

1. Research
2. Value Proposition
3. Questions
4. Advances
5. Unexpected Value
6. Agenda

Element #1 – Research

The process of gathering, analyzing, and interpreting information about your prospect – their drivers and characteristics, market and sub-markets, challenges and financial status, goals and objectives, the particulars about this potential opportunity including other alternatives or solutions they may be considering – is the homework you do before your meeting.

As you research, consider:

- In what industry, market, and sub-market is your prospective client?
- What types of clients do they have?
- What are the drivers in their industry right now?
- What is their financial status?
- What are their goals and objectives?

Consider their current situation:

- What are the challenges regarding their current situation?
- What is the potential impact of those challenges?
- What hidden challenges might they encounter?
- What might the impact of those hidden challenges be?
- What risks are likely to be of greatest concern to them?
- What fears might they be feeling about a making a bad decision?

Consider the importance of each specific issue:
- What are the specific issues this client is facing?
- How great is the impact of each specific issue?
- What is their priority for resolving each specific issue?

Consider their decision-making process:
- Who will be involved in making the decision?
- What evaluation processes will they go through?
- Where are they in the process now?
- What have they accomplished up to this point?
- What is their deadline to make a decision?
- What are the drivers behind the timing of their decision?
- What criteria will they use to determine their ultimate solution?
- How will they go about making their final decision?
- What other solutions or alternatives are they or might they be considering?
- What are the pros and cons of those possible solutions?

Consider the resources and constraints they may be facing:
- Who on their team will be involved in implementing the project?
- What thought has been given to a budget for the results they are seeking?
- What has kept them from solving this problem already?
- What other improvement opportunities might they have overlooked?

Then, consider any additional research you might need to conduct before your meeting. Online tools include:
- The customer's website
- Google searches
- Google alerts
- RSS feeds
- LinkedIn, Twitter, Facebook and other social media platforms
- Industry-specific websites and databases
- EDGAR (the SEC's Electronic Data Gathering, Analysis & Retrieval system) and publicly traded company resources

---

EXERCISE #30 - Researching Accounts

Instructions: Using the tools you've learned and the questions from the section above, research your highest priority account using the form on page 146 in Free Additional Resources. Download additional copies at PureMuir.com/TPCworkbook and perform this activity for all of your priority accounts.

Group Discussion: Break into groups of 3-4 and share what you discovered during your research. What information did you uncover? What opportunities or challenges does that suggest? What gaps of information did you uncover? What questions do you plan to ask when given the opportunity?

Each group decides what research tools proved to be the most helpful and writes them on a flipchart or whiteboard. Then each group takes turns sharing their list with the entire group and why they found them most valuable.

Element #2 – Value Proposition

This is the answer to, "Why should this prospect see me?" It describes what about your offer is of benefit to your prospective client. It is the measurable value you bring. If you have not met with your prospect before, then you will have a value hypothesis or best guess as to what will benefit them. Your value proposition is the primary factor that determines how you are positioned with this prospect. At the minimum your value proposition will have a metric (a measurable performance indicator), a direction (does it increase it or lower it), and magnitude (how much it affects the metric).

Things to consider for your value proposition:
- Why should this prospect see me now? What is my value hypothesis?
- What tangible value can I bring to this client?
- What are the metrics that measure the value I bring?
- What is the magnitude of the value I bring?
- What evidence do I have that I can help?

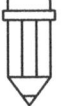

EXERCISE #31 - Determining & Monetizing Your Value Proposition - Part 1

Your value proposition answers the question, "Why should this client see me?"

Instructions: Leverage the work you've already completed with Exercises #19 - Your Industry Metrics (pg. 57), #20 - Crafting Value Propositions (pg. 59), and #21 - Applying Your Value Proposition to Your Upcoming Appointments (pg. 61).

Client/Prospect: _____

Why should this client see me now? What is my value hypothesis?

What tangible value can I bring to this client?

What are the key metrics that measure the value I bring?

What is the magnitude of the value I can bring? (how much)

What evidence do I have that I can help?

EXERCISE #31 - Determining & Monetizing Your Value Proposition - Part 2

Instructions: Using your answers in Part 1 complete the matrix on page 102. Refer to the two examples to get you started. If you have not uncovered your prospect's actual values through research or discovery, use estimated values and make getting these actual values a priority during your next encounter.

Metric – Measures the tangible value of your solution.

Current Value – Current or estimated value of this metric for this client.

Desired Value – Using the same metric, enter the value desired or the realistic improvement obtainable by implementing your solution.

Value of Difference – Subtract Current Value from Desired Value (or obtainable value) to determine the difference.

Value Over Time – Now calculate the total value improvement over a realistic period of time. (example: 5 years) This is the total accumulated value your solution might create over time.

As you calculate the value of the difference and the value over time you will likely need to use other important metrics to complete the calculation. Leverage your understanding of how your solution affects positive change and the mechanics involved to use the appropriate metrics to calculate value.

Example Metrics for Sales:

Metric	Current Value	Desired Value	Value of Difference	Value Over Time
Sales Revenue	$12.5M/ yr.	$16M/ yr.	$3.5M	$3.5M * 5 yrs. = $17.5M
Close Ratio	26%	32%	Pipeline Value = $48M Value of Percentage Difference = 6% (32% - 26% = 6%) Value of Increase = $2.88M ($48M * 6% = $2.88M)	$2.88M * 5 yrs. = $14.4M Additional Sales Revenue
Close Ratio Effect on Commission	26%	32%	Average Commission = 5% Average Sale = $250K Individual Pipeline = $8M Value of Percentage Difference = 6% (32% - 26% = 6%) Sales Revenue Increase = $480K ($8M * 6% = $480K) Sales Commission Increase = $24K ($480K * 5% = $24K)	$24K * 5 yrs. = $120K Additional Personal Income (with no required increase in pipeline)

Example Metrics for Accounts Receivable:

Metric	Current Value	Desired Value	Value of Difference	Value Over Time
Days Sales Outstanding (DSO)	92%	98%	Value of Percentage Difference = 6% Total Accounts Receivable = $89,500,000 Value of Improvement = $5,370,000 (Total Accounts Receivable * 6% = $5,370,000)	$5,370,000 * 5 years = $26,850,000
Bad Debt Percentage	11%	4%	Value of Percentage Difference = 7% Total Accounts Receivable = $89,500,000 Value of the Improvement = $6,265,000 ($89,500,000 * 7% = $6,265,000)	$6,265,000 * 5 years = $31,325,000

Client/Prospect: _____

Metric	Current Value	Desired Value	Value of Difference	Value Over Time

 Group Discussion: Break into groups of 3-4 and share what you discovered during your research. What is your value hypothesis for your next 1-5 encounters? What is the potential value over time? What gaps of information did you uncover? What questions do you plan to ask when given the opportunity?

Each group decides one opportunity and its value hypothesis to share with the entire group. Write the opportunity and metrics on a flipchart or whiteboard. Then each group takes turns sharing the chosen opportunity with the entire group.

Element #3 – Questions

The information gathering and value-adding questions you intend to ask should be developed prior to your encounter. True value-adding questions are those to which the client does not already know the answer. They require thought, encourage reflection, and advance the conversation into new territory. When we prompt our prospect's higher-level thinking we are literally adding value. Asking tough, powerful questions define you as a consultant and communicate that you have a genuine intent to help. You should prepare two or three high-value questions for every encounter.

Consider the following when developing questions:

- What additional information do I need that has not been answered by my research?
- What information-gathering questions do I intend to ask the client?
- What is the priority of each question? If I'm not able to ask all my questions, which should I ask first?
- What value-add questions do I intend to ask?
- What questions can I ask that will stimulate and facilitate my prospect's understanding?

# EXERCISE #32 - Preparing Questions

Instructions: For your same upcoming sales encounter, use the form below to identify the questions you need to ask and prioritize them. Then leverage the work already completed on page 88 with Exercise #27 - Powerful Questions (part 4) to create three powerful Value-Add Questions for each encounter and prioritize them.

Client/Prospect: _____

Information-Gathering Questions: What additional information do I need?	Priority

Value-Add Questions: What questions can I ask that will stimulate and facilitate my client's understanding?	Priority

Group Discussion: Break into groups of 3-4 and share your questions. Time with clients is precious and limited. Can the answers to your information-gathering questions be found elsewhere? Are your Value-Add Questions actually adding value? Do they stimulate new thinking and increase understanding?

Each group picks one opportunity and then reviews the questions with the entire group.

Element #4 – Advances

Planned advances answer, "What do I want my prospect to do as a result of this meeting?" It is the action(s) you want them to take. An ideal advance is the highest level of commitment you can reasonably expect them to make as a result of this encounter. Advances should be specific and measurable, center on the action the prospect will take, move the sale forward, and be reasonable from their perspective. Plan an ideal advance and several alternate advances if your ideal proves unrealistic.

Your ideal advance:
- What is my primary call objective?
- Is my primary call objective specific and measurable? Does it center on the action the client will take; move the sale forward; Is it reasonable from the buyer's perspective?
- Once I learn The Perfect Close phrase how will I use it to obtain this advance?

Alternate/additional advances if you're unable to achieve your ideal advance, or if the meeting is going extremely well:
- What are my secondary/backup objectives for this meeting?
- What alternate or additional advances could I request as a result of this meeting?
- Once I learn The Perfect Close phrase how will I use it for each of these?

Consider the minimum advance you are willing to settle for:
- What is the smallest advance I am willing to accept and still move forward?
- Once I learn The Perfect Close phrase how will I use it to obtain this advance?

 ## EXERCISE #33 - Planning Advances

Your planned advances answer the question, "What do I want my prospect to do as a result of this meeting?"

Instructions: For your upcoming sales encounter, identify your Primary Call Objective, Ideal Advance and Alternate/Backup Advances. Leverage the work on page 64 Exercise #22 – What Do I Want My Client to Do?

Remember: Call Objectives should be 1. Specific & measurable. 2. Center on the action the client will take. 3. Move the sales forward. 4. Reasonable from the client's perspective.

Ask yourself, "Which of these is the minimum Advance I am willing to settle for and continue to engage in this opportunity?"

Client/Prospect: _____

Primary Call Objective
Ideal Advance

Secondary / Backup Objectives
Alternate / Backup Advances

Group Discussion: Break into groups of 3-4 and share your Call Objectives and Advances. Do your Call Objectives meet the four criteria? What is the minimum Advance you are willing to settle for?

Each group picks one encounter to share with the group and then reviews the Primary Call Objective, Ideal Advance and Alternate/Backup Advances with the entire group.

Element #5 – Unexpected Value

This is the unanticipated value your prospect receives as a result of your meeting and should be delivered on every sales encounter. Delivering insight is the primary way you add value, but you can also ask powerful questions; facilitate understanding; help clients see the path to success; share new ideas and tips; deliver education; share news, trigger events and insights about their industry.

Ask yourself, "What unexpected value will I bring to this meeting?"

EXERCISE #34 - Unexpected Value

Unexpected Value is the unanticipated value your prospect receives as a result of your meeting.

Instructions: For your next 1-5 sales encounters or target accounts, leverage the brainstorming you did in on page 95 with Exercise #29 - Adding Value To Each Encounter to identify and plan the Unexpected Value you will deliver for each meeting.

Unexpected Value
Meeting 1 - Client/Prospect:
Meeting 2 - Client/Prospect:
Meeting 3 - Client/Prospect:
Meeting 4 - Client/Prospect:
Meeting 5 - Client/Prospect:

Group Discussion: Break into groups of 3-4 and share the Unexpected Value you plan to bring to your next few appointments. Does the Unexpected Value help identify an unanticipated solution, an unrecognized problem, unseen opportunity or add value in one of the key seven areas?

Deliver Insight
Employ Powerful Questions
Help Them Better Understand Their Needs
Help Them See the Path to Success

Share New Ideas
Deliver Education
Share News, Trigger Events, and Insights from Their Industry

Each member of the group selects their top answer and writes it on the flipchart or whiteboard then each group shares their list with the entire group.

Element #6 – Agenda

This is the list of items to be discussed during your meeting. The prospect's stated interests should be the main focus. Confirm your agenda with them and make sure it meets their expectation of what they want covered. You should have an agenda for every encounter. You will learn more about what makes an effective agenda in the following chapter.

For your agenda, consider the purpose of the meeting:
- What is the meeting's primary purpose from my prospect's perspective?
- What specific directives or expectations does my prospect have for this meeting?

Consider those in attendance:
- Who from my team will join me?
- Who from my prospect's organization will (or should be) in attendance?
- What are their names and titles?
- What will be each participant's objectives?

Consider your initial comments and interactions:
- What will your opening comment be?
- What will you state as the purpose of your meeting?
- What new introductions are needed (either on the prospect's team or your own)?
- How will you summarize your understanding of the prospect's current situation and challenges?

Consider your positioning:
- What strengths do I bring to this opportunity?
- What might the prospect consider to be my vulnerabilities?
- What can I do or say to increase my credibility with them?

Consider the physical logistics:
- What is the proposed date, time, and estimated length?
- Where will the meeting take place and in what format?
- Who on the client's side is coordinating the meeting?
- Have all of the details of the meeting been confirmed?
- Have all the materials needed for the meeting been confirmed?
- Have attendee schedules been checked?
- What time do you need to begin wrapping up?

EXERCISE #35 - Agenda

Instructions: Using the previous priming questions and a blank sheet of paper (or whatever agenda template you normally use), draft a brief agenda for your next 1-5 sales appointments.

The meeting is not about you.
Make the meeting inherently valuable for your client.

Resources
Download blank PDFs of all planning forms at PureMuir.com/TPCworkbook.

Sales Encounter Planning Form
Once your research is complete you will be ready to plan your sales encounter. Your awareness of gaps in your research and the need for additional information will help formulate the questions you will ask. Remember, the meeting is not all about you. It is important that you make the meeting inherently valuable for your client. Your research will help you do that.

Conclusion
Using a planning process will greatly improve the effectiveness of your meetings. More effective meetings will solidify your credibility, perceived authority, and differentiate you from your competition. More effective meetings will lead to your clients achieving their desired solutions while you enjoy higher close ratios, more closed opportunities, and greater personal success.

Follow my straightforward checklist of planning steps, and you will be able to repeat your success over and over again.

Next up, we will discover how to create an effective agenda that will maximize the value and impact of each meeting.

CHAPTER 12

Leveraging Agendas for Effective Sales Encounters

Meeting agendas are far more powerful than most people realize. They mitigate risk and greatly improve the likelihood that each meeting will have the outcome you desire.

Agendas provide nine important functions:

1. Position you as a true professional and advisor
2. Heighten the importance of your meeting
3. Define the meeting's objectives
4. Show potential attendees why it's important to attend
5. Set expectations
6. Help invitees prepare
7. Provide structure and sequence to the meeting
8. Dedicate time to establish action items and next steps
9. Provide a way to measure the success of the meeting

A solid agenda ensures that the time invested in the meeting has a valuable return for everyone involved. Your goals are to obtain your ideal advance and deliver your prospect both edification and unexpected value. The best way to achieve this win-win dynamic is to collaborate with your client on the agenda.

Collaborating with your client or prospect on the agenda achieves a three-fold purpose:

1. It ensures you don't overlook any key objectives.
2. It ensures the depth and duration of each item stays within the meeting's overall timeframe.
3. It increases buy-in from attendees who have a hand in designing the meeting.

By asking for input from your prospect along with their key staff members, departments, and managers who should be involved, the likelihood of your success increases dramatically. Their input, combined with yours, regarding topics to include and how much time should be devoted to each will garner greater attendance, acceptance, and support for your meeting.

In complex sales where many parties may be involved, start the process well in advance. The more people involved, the longer the process can take. Do not wait until the last minute to formulate a collaborative agenda, which can easily take a week to complete. As soon as you're aware that a meeting is needed, begin the process of formulating an agenda with your prospect.

It's a good thing if the prospect actively adds agenda items. Let them share. Sometimes this can result in too many agenda items for the allotted time, so you may need to carefully consider their input and narrow the focus to a manageable agenda. Acknowledge the importance of the tabled items and set up another meeting to cover them.

As you revise the agenda, share updates and changes with your contact and other people involved to ensure it still makes sense.

Here are the functions of your meeting agenda.

Agendas Position You as a True Professional and Advisor

Your agenda is a reflection of you, your company, and your professionalism. Clients and prospects alike will project much about the value of the meeting and your professionalism from the quality of your agenda. Make sure it looks professional.

Simplicity is key. Your agenda should fit on a single sheet of paper, and should be easy to follow at a glance. Maintain a meeting agenda template to get you started. Find several agenda templates at PureMuir.com/TPCworkbook.

Clients and prospects alike will project much about the value of the meeting and your professionalism from the quality of your agenda.

If you have attachments for the agenda (e.g., reports, documents, images, etc.), include them in your email and consider putting them online via secure hyperlink so attendees can access them. If they are not needed prior to the meeting, simply distribute a hard copy at the meeting.

Agendas Add Importance to Your Meeting

The existence of a formal agenda automatically increases your prospect's perceived importance of your meeting. One of my C-level executive friends requires a written agenda to determine whether or not he will attend any given meeting, saying, "If it's not important enough to have a written agenda, it's not important enough for me to attend."

Agendas Define the Objective(s) of the Meeting

The meeting objective drives everything else. It shows each attendee why it's important to attend, sets expectations as to what the meeting will accomplish, helps prospects prepare, and provides a way to determine the meeting's effectiveness. If you're not sure why you are meeting, chances are your stakeholders won't know either.

By defining a meeting objective you are far more likely to get the attendance you need and, more importantly, the acceptance you need for your solution. Identify all stakeholders that should be involved and consider what their personal objectives might be (they may not always be in alignment with you or other attendees). Understanding each stakeholder's personal objectives will greatly improve your stated meeting objective. Remember, companies don't buy things – people do.

The meeting objective should be stated from the prospect's perspective and focused on the outcomes they hope to achieve – their expressed interests, challenges, goals, etc. – not yours. Although we have our own objectives for the meeting, there should be no focus on our products and services, only the outcomes they hope to achieve by utilizing those things.

If possible, craft a meeting objective that is broad enough to interest all attendees. The narrower your audience, the easier this is. For example, if your attendees are 100% IT staff, then your stated objective can be narrowed to technical issues. However, when your audience includes executive management, finance, IT, operations, the legal department, and field personnel zoom out and consider the outcomes important to everyone.

To sum up, your stated meeting objective should:
1. Be from the prospect's perspective.
2. Focus on the outcomes they hope to achieve.
3. Be broad enough interest all attendees.

Examples of stated meeting objectives:
- Explore best practices for growing business despite challenges with lower customer engagement.
- Review & discuss implications & trade-off of 100% cloud deployment.
- Discuss strategies for preparing for value-based reimbursement.
- Review practical steps for reducing risk & simplifying regulatory compliance issues.
- Scrutinize the implications of upgrading solutions & how to successfully implement organizational change.
- Review & discuss strategies for preparing for reimbursement models that place a greater share of financial risk on the organization.
- Examine the top 5 strategies for reducing operational costs while maintaining quality.
- Discuss the current options for reducing claim denial losses in the context of regulatory change.
- Evaluate the financial & operational implications of recent regulation & how to best address them.

- Analyze strategies for reducing executive & employee workload while improving quality.
- Evaluate technical specifications & tradeoffs of deployment models.
- Determine & decide which approach is best for [ABC Co.].
- Discuss & finalize agreement terms & conditions.

Notice the first word in each example is a verb. My favorite is "Discuss" because it implies collaboration. Here are some other words you will find useful for phrasing your meeting objective:

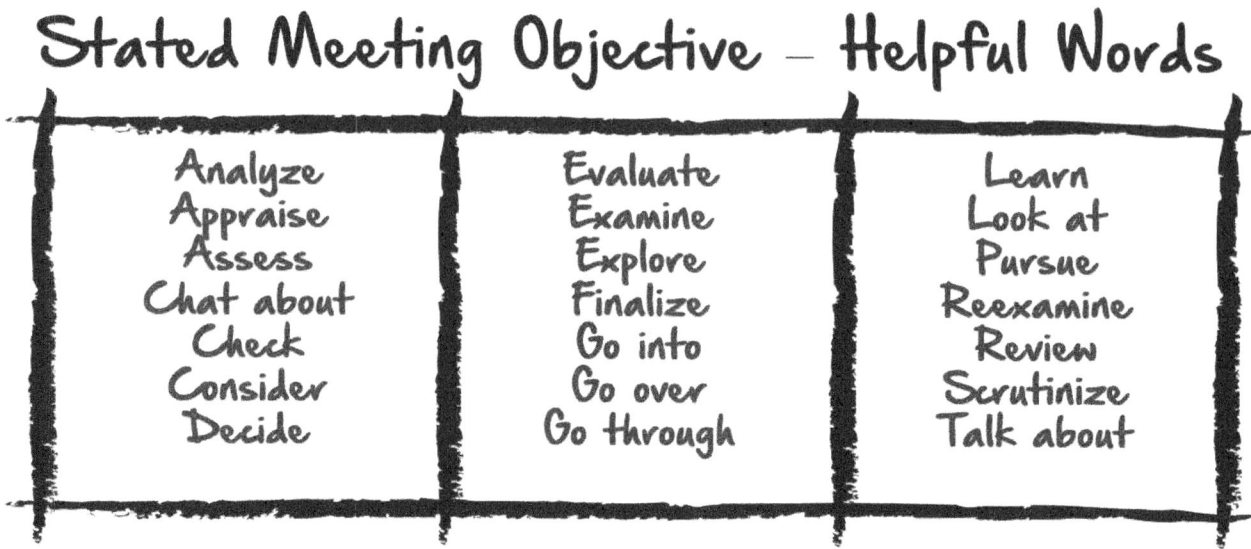

Stated meeting objectives help you plan, and stating it from the prospect's perspective helps you plan the meeting in a way that adds value for them. The more concrete your meeting objectives, the more focused your agenda will be. It also suggests what questions and issues may arise and will help you be more prepared for these discussions when they happen.

 **EXERCISE #36** - **Stated Meeting Objective - Part 1**

Stated Meeting Objectives show each attendee why it's important to attend, sets expectations as to what the meeting will accomplish, helps you and the client prepare, and provides a way to determine the meeting's effectiveness.

Instructions: For your next 1-5 appointments, use the form below to create a Stated Meeting Objective. Each Stated Meeting Objective should:

Be stated from the prospect's perspective.

Focus on the outcomes they hope to achieve.

Be broad enough to be of interest to all attendees.

Stated Meeting Objective
Meeting 1 - Client/Prospect:
Meeting 2 - Client/Prospect:
Meeting 3 - Client/Prospect:
Meeting 4 - Client/Prospect:
Meeting 5 - Client/Prospect:

Agendas Show Potential Attendees Why They Should Attend

The worst thing that can happen is poor attendance. Progress cannot be made if the right people do not attend. Meeting value, like beauty, is in the eye of the beholder. Until we articulate the value of the meeting in our agenda, potential attendees will assume your meeting, like most corporate meetings, will be a typical waste of time.

By outlining the purpose, discussion topics, and its time frame potential attendees can easily determine whether or not they should attend. The best way to do this is to explicitly state what the outcome objective is. Tie the outcome to their important objectives, and attendees will make space on their calendar for your meeting – which is tremendously beneficial because you will have the right people in the room to help your initiative succeed. This alone can shorten your sales cycle. Having key individuals attend or not attend can make and break sales.

The right attendance also provides a measure of risk control after the sale is complete. Stakeholders who participate in the evaluation stages are more likely to feel their concerns were listened to, that they influenced the decision, and that their needs were addressed. This higher level of communication and participation reduces possible negative reactions to future, unforeseen incidents.

If your solution requires dramatic change for your prospect, send your agenda in advance to familiarize stakeholders prior to your meeting which helps eliminate possible surprise responses when they learn things for the first time during your meeting.

Agendas Set the Client's Expectations

Have you ever attended a meeting where a party's interests were not addressed, and that created problems? Domineering stakeholders completely derail meetings by repeatedly inserting their personal agenda. This can be especially challenging when the domineering party is a high-ranking official.

With a collaborative agenda, sent in advance, everyone's expectations regarding the meeting's purpose and the topics to be addressed are clearly defined. It doesn't guarantee that someone won't try and hijack your meeting, but it does reduce the chances, and it allows you to say something like, "Those are all good points. The purpose of this meeting is to X. We plan to cover those other points in an upcoming meeting." I have used this many times to reel-in high ranking officials who were not adequately briefed on the purpose of the meeting, and it works very well.

Meeting Agendas Help Your Invitees Prepare

Attendees can prepare when they know the meeting's purpose and topics in advance. Meetings that require specific data can stall without that information, but agendas, sent in advance, eliminate situations where participants aren't ready to discuss a subject because they didn't know facts or figures were going to be covered. Consider including an "Information Required" section on your agenda so invitees will clearly see details needed in order to have a productive meeting. If appropriate, suggest (with the assistance of your prospect) assigning someone to provide the information. When specific individuals are made responsible for their participation, the meeting will take on new significance for those participants.

Of course, agendas also prepare you. Your level of preparedness will directly translate to the meeting's degree of success.

# EXERCISE #36 - Stated Meeting Objective - Part 2

Instructions: Using the Stated Meeting Objectives you just created in Part 1, complete the following matrix.

Stated Meeting Objective – Your Stated Meeting Objective goes here.

Shows Why They Should Attend – Answer Yes or No

Sets the Right Expectation – Answer Yes or No

What information/homework should your prospect prepare? – List items attendees should prepare/complete in advance to get maximum value for your meeting.

Stated Meeting Objective	Shows Why They Should Attend? (Y/N)	Sets the Right Expectations?	What information/homework should your prospect prepare?

Group Discussion: Break into groups of 3-4. Share your Stated Meeting Objectives with the group. Is each one stated from the prospect's perspective? Does it focus on the outcomes they hope to achieve? Is it broad enough to be of interest to all attendees?

Each member selects their top answer and writes it on the flipchart or whiteboard then each group shares their list with the entire group.

Agendas Provide the Meeting's Structure and Sequence

Agendas identify specific topics for discussion, prevent others from adding new issues at the meeting, eliminate guesswork as to whether a particular issue will be discussed, and keep everyone focused in ways that simple verbal guidance cannot. Essentially, it's a roadmap guiding participants through what needs to be accomplished and encouraging them to stay on track while driving the conversation toward conclusion.

Make your agenda specific enough to elicit adequate preparation and intelligent discussion. If it's too broad, attendees may not be prepared to adequately drill into the subject matter. The content must be relevant to all participants and within their framework of understanding. If items are beyond the understanding of certain participants, you will lose their attention. Conversely, if content is overly simplistic, attendees may resort to texting or checking email during your meeting.

There is no one-size-fits-all meeting agenda. While templates can get us started, each agenda should be tailored to the meeting's specific objectives. Jumpstart your process, download several agenda templates at PureMuir.com/TPCworkbook.

Structurally, every agenda should contain the following elements (though the exact items and wording should be tailored from meeting to meeting):

1. Logistics - Date, start and end times, location, a title, list of invited attendees
2. Meeting Objectives - A single sentence, if possible, stating the purpose of the meeting and its specific desired outcome (a decision or action item) a. From the client's perspective; b. Focused on the outcomes they hope to achieve; c. Broad enough to be of interest to all attendees.
3. Housekeeping - Welcomes and introductions, accommodations regarding food, bathrooms, parking validation, etc. You may also choose to do an agenda overview before jumping into the first item.
4. Items - The "meat" of your agenda that communicates the topics to be discussed, in the appropriate sequence, and serves to keep your meeting on track.

    The sequence, or order, can make a big difference as you are, in effect, prioritizing items. It is a good idea to front-load the meeting with the highest priority topics, so if the meeting is cut short the most critical items will have been addressed and less important items can wait for a follow-up meeting.

    The sequence orients attendees to the flow of the meeting and offers them a sense of progress as you step through items. It also allows you to maintain order, since participants anxious to cover a particular item can see it's coming up. If someone is to lead a discussion item, note this on the agenda, so they can anticipate the preparation and timing involved.

    Similarly, with the mutually agreed-upon agenda as your guide, you can prevent getting bogged down in any one area. When you see this phenomenon developing, "parking lot" the topic and continue moving forward in the interest of sticking to the agenda and keeping the meeting on schedule.

    A timed agenda can be especially helpful since a ticking clock is motivating, and you can move on to the next item when the allotted time is up. If you suspect that time may get away from you, include a written time frame for each item. Even if you don't put this in writing, estimate the time you'll need for each topic so you're able to keep your meeting on schedule.

    However, it is important to be both disciplined and flexible. Approach your meeting with the intent to adhere to the structure and timings, but if the conversation is highly beneficial, don't be afraid to let it run long. Likewise, if the conversation is dragging or rehashing, use the agenda productively to move on. The framework of the agenda gives you the Zen-like ability to expand or contract as well as stay on or move outside the structure in whatever way is most valuable for everyone involved.

5. Next Steps/Action Items – Your opportunity at the end of the meeting to determine action items that will keep the project moving forward. Have your ideal advance and secondary/backup advances planned. This is when you'll use your pre-planned Perfect Close phrase (which you are about to learn). Discuss all action items and next steps and determine:
    a. What needs to be done
    b. To whom it is assigned

    c. The target timeframe to complete it

       This is also the time to schedule the next meeting date. In addition, consider including an "outcome agenda" in which you briefly note subsequent agenda items and the outcomes sought for those topics. This can be amazingly effective, especially when they require decisions or consensus on previous agenda items.

Remember to weave your own call objective and unexpected value into the agenda. In most cases prospects are not open to receiving unexpected value until their main issues have been addressed, so it is generally best to include that value toward the middle or end of your agenda. Be careful not to telegraph your unexpected value on the agenda, or even worse, turn it into an expectation. It should be just what it's called – unexpected value.

The meeting is a win-win when both you and your prospect have met your objectives.

EXERCISE #37 - Creating Agendas

Instructions: For your next priority meeting, use the Meeting Planner form on page 150 in Free Additional Resources to plan your agenda. Include all the necessary elements. Download additional copies at PureMuir.com/TPCworkbook

Group Discussion: Break into groups of 3-4 and share the agendas you have created. Are all the essential elements included? Does it include a plan to deliver Unexpected Value? Does it include Next Steps/Action Items? What ideas that others used could you incorporate into your agenda to make it more valuable?

Agendas Provide Time to Establish Action Items and Next steps

As outlined above, to facilitate and affect positive change for your prospects and keep their project moving forward, it is vital to allow adequate time toward the end of your agenda to establish action items and next steps.

Business meetings are infamous for being unproductive. Don't let yours become another casualty in the pile of dead meetings at the corporate assembly graveyard. The number-one complaint about most meetings is "nothing was accomplished." Make sure something does get accomplished by allocating time to establish next steps and action items. When the meeting arrives at this item, thank the participants for the valuable discussion and address any obvious action items that have arisen during the course of the meeting, then work through the next steps. Be careful to define:

- What needs to be done
- To whom it is assigned (you or the prospect and which person specifically owns it)
- The target time frame to complete it

Sometimes, sales reps have concerns about committing prospective clients to completion dates for action items or next steps. Relax. Simply ask something like, "When should I check back with you on X?" That will establish your target timeframe.

Get commitment on your ideal advance as well as secondary or fall-back advances which, of course, you will have defined prior to even creating the agenda. After addressing the obvious action items, you will use The Perfect Close for your ideal advance. Regardless of their answer, follow up by suggesting one of your secondary or fall-back advances and repeat as needed. This will make more sense after the next chapter.

> **It is vital that you allow time in your agenda to establish action items and next steps.**

This is, literally, the most important part of the meeting for you. In the next chapter, you'll see how facilitative and non-confrontational this step will become. Your prospects expect you to help them make the positive changes that will bring about their desired results; they expect you to encourage them to become better than they are. Push your clients and prospects toward improvement. Be their coach and guide them through each little commitment it takes to achieve their goals.

This is more than you advancing your sale. This is leadership. Few people have true mentors and leaders in their life, so guide them along the path that leads them to improvement – however challenging, difficult, or narrow in its scope – and they will thank you.

> **This is more than you advancing your sale. This is leadership.**

In your excitement of getting commitments to your planned advances, don't forget, while everyone is still present, to schedule the next meeting. If it disperses without setting the next date, it will make it much harder to schedule the next meeting. If your request is met with any uncertainty, suggest to "pencil in a date" which can always be changed later. This ensures that you have commitment for further collaboration.

Always end every meeting with:

1. A review of the agreed-upon action items, and
2. The date for the next meeting

Follow up in an email to the attendees. Thank them for the productive meeting, summarize what was discussed, list the action item assignments and deadlines, confirm the next meeting date, and begin the collaborative process of creating the next agenda. This is professional and ensures that everyone is on the same page.

> **Always end every meeting with a review of the agreed upon action items and the date for the next meeting.**

EXERCISE #38 - Making Meetings Measurable

Instructions: Consider your last few meetings. Using the matrix below score each meeting on a scale of 1 (weak) to 5 (strong) in each area.

Client Name / Date	If asked by another person, my customer would describe our meeting as valuable.	I accomplished my ideal advance.	I accomplished one or more of my alternative advances.	I regard this meeting as a success.

Group Discussion: Break into groups of 3-4 and discuss your previous appointments and how you scored them. What would you change given the chance to go back in time and do the meeting again? What changes does that suggest going forward?

Agendas Provide a Way to Measure the Success of Your Meeting

We want everyone to walk out of the meeting thinking, "Man, that was a good meeting! I'm glad I attended." Agendas with a stated meeting objective provide an excellent way to judge whether or not the meeting achieved its goal.

Because you planned your meeting with an ideal advance as well as secondary/backup advances, it's simple to measure its success. Did you accomplish your call objectives? Did the client achieve theirs? Why or why not? Is another meeting required? Setting call objectives allows you to continuously improve the effectiveness of your meetings.

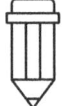 **CLOSING SECRET** - Agendas are powerful tools that greatly improve the likelihood that each meeting will have the outcome you desire.

 EXERCISE #39 - Agenda Review

Instructions: If possible, break into groups of 3-4 and refer back to the Agendas created in Chapter 11 Exercise #35 (pg. 109). Compare those to your newly created agendas. Discuss the differences. Will the new agendas be more effective? What was missing from the first set of agendas? What was the most valuable thing you discovered?

Each group writes their top discoveries on a flipchart or whiteboard and shares with the entire group.

Conclusion

It is unprofessional to not have a meeting agenda and sends the message that you are a time-waster, not a value creator. Agendas are far more powerful than most people realize. A well-crafted agenda will have a strong effect on the meeting's outcome, and it can exert influence before the meeting even happens.

Meeting agendas produce a tremendous return for a modest investment of time and greatly improve effectiveness. They provide a logical and natural way to advance the sale and lead them toward their goals. Show them each commitment is a step in the right direction. Encourage and challenge them to take action. When they have accomplished their objective they will be grateful, thankful, and will credit you as a contributor to their success. This is the sweet spot of selling.

CHAPTER 13

The Perfect Close

"If the language you use to close makes you uncomfortable, then it probably isn't good closing language."

– Anthony Iannarino

The Perfect Close is simple. You only need to learn two questions, and most of the time, you only need to use one of them. There is an initial question and a follow-up question. In addition to learning how to apply these two questions, it is helpful to know some logical advances for your prospective client. It's not required, but it helps.

Here are the questions:

Initial Question: "Does it make sense for us to X?"

Follow-Up Question: "What is a good next step?"

Simple, huh? Let's examine question one: "Does it make sense for us to X?"

In this case the "X" is a logical advance for your sale.

Here are some examples:

- "Does it make sense to talk about scheduling a site visit for you, so you can see the product in a live environment?"
- "Does it make sense for us to talk about putting together a financial assessment of your current situation?"
- "Does it make sense for us to talk about getting your credit approved while we go through the other details together?"
- "Does it make sense for us to talk about putting together some samples, so you can try them out?"
- "Does it make sense for us to schedule some time with our creative department to give you some ideas on what your options might be?"
- "Does it make sense for us to talk about doing a workflow analysis, so we can see where the best efficiencies can be gained?"
- "Does it make sense for us to put together a statement of work for you, so we can start getting an idea of the project's scope?"
- "Does it make sense for us to schedule an appraiser to check out the property, so we can get an idea of its market value?"
- "Does it make sense for us to schedule a physical for you, so we can see what kind of rates we can get?"
- "Does it make sense for us to put together a proposal for you, so we can start sizing up the investment?"
- "Does it make sense for us to schedule a meeting with your team, so we can get their input on what would be most beneficial for them?"
- "Does it make sense for us to schedule some time with our technical team, so we can get a clearer picture of the requirements?"
- "Does it make sense for me to meet your executive sponsor, so we can get some specifics about her objectives for the project?"
- "Does it make sense for us to schedule a demonstration, so your whole team can see it in action?"
- "Does it make sense for us to talk about wrapping everything up?"

The Nuances of Question One

The stem of, "Does it make sense…," is so simple you might overlook its sublime power. Many salespeople new to the phrasing misinterpret the question and get it wrong. Despite being called The Perfect Close, the question is not really a closing question.

"Does it make sense?" ≠ "Will you buy?"

"Does it make sense…" is not:

- Will you buy?
- Will you X? (i.e. do something)
- Do you want it in green or blue? (loaded)
- Customer: Do you have it in X? Seller: Would you buy it if we had it in X?
- This is the perfect time to move forward, isn't it? (manipulative)
- This offer ends today. You don't want to miss out, do you? (manipulative)
- Where do you want it shipped? (assumed)
- If I can do X will you buy today?
- Shall we get started on the contract?

Question one of The Perfect Close is nowhere near an ultimatum. We are not asking our client to DO anything. We are simply asking if a given thing (your advance) makes sense.

At its core, question one is really a timing question. We are asking if the timing is right to do something. In fact, it's a perfectly acceptable variation of, "Bob, is the timing right for us to talk about scheduling a site visit for you and your team?" After years of application and teaching it to others, I prefer, "Does it make sense…" because it is easier to remember and more universal in its application. Both are fine. If the "timing" phrase feels more natural for you, use it.

But, there is a subtle but absolutely critical difference between asking our client to do something and asking if it makes sense to do something. Here's the difference:

Differences between traditional closes & The Perfect Close

Will you X?	Does it make sense to X?
Yes/No question on a single course of action.	Cannot reject the course of action—only the timing of it.
Timed improperly, creates pressure and tension.	Eliminates the pressure and tension risk of improperly timed questions (because it is a timing question).
May cause clients to view you as pushy and limit future communications.	Eliminates the risk that clients may see you as pushy. Keeps clients communicating throughout their buying process.
Leaves you at square one if the reply is no.	Sets up your follow-up question (question 2) if the reply is negative.
Reveals little to nothing about where the client is in their buying process.	Reveals much about where the client is within their buying process.
	Paces the sale at the rate the customer is ready to go.
	Feels facilitative to clients and makes them feel in control.

🗝 **CLOSING SECRET** - By asking a timing question prospects cannot reject you or your course of action, only the timing of it.

The most important distinction is that when you ask a client to do something in a polar or binary fashion (i.e. Will you X?), they are forced into a yes/no response. It is wonderful when they say "yes," but when a client answers negatively, they have officially rejected our advance, and that leaves us back at square one. Moreover, depending on the request and how far we are mismatched with the client, there is a heightened risk that they will perceive us as pushy or self-serving (even if that is not our intention). Then, they throttle back their communication and the information they share with us, perhaps altogether.

Contrast this with question one of The Perfect Close. When we ask if "it makes sense" to do something, we are not actually asking them to take that step yet, but they can clearly see that is the direction we are heading. If they reply negatively, they are not rejecting the course of action, rather they are only rejecting its timing. Because it is a timing question this leaves you and the client emotionally on much higher ground and prevents you from being considered pushy.

🗝 **CLOSING SECRET** - When we ask if something "makes sense" we are not asking them to do anything, but they can clearly see that is the direction we are heading.

Telegraphing Your Request

- When asking clients if it "makes sense" to do something, we're not actually asking them to take that step yet, but they can clearly see that's the direction we're heading.
- We are telegraphing our request.
- Regardless of the answer it leaves us on emotionally higher ground.
- Because it's a timing question, we have more options, and it sets up question two.
- These are subtle and important differences between question one, and traditional closing methods.
- That makes it better.

🗝 **CLOSING SECRET** - Regardless of a client's answer, The Perfect Close questions leave you and your client emotionally on much higher ground.

It is impossible to get the timing of this question wrong precisely because it <u>is</u> a timing question. This keeps clients communicating freely throughout the process and paces the sale at the rate they are ready to go which improves their experience and makes them feel more in control while perceiving you as a facilitator.

Your client's response to question one (your ideal advance) reveals much about where they are in their buying cycle. If they decline the timing of a modest or an extremely logical advance, then it is an indicator to us that we have missed something. Because we didn't actually ask them to make a commitment (as with other types of closes), we still have options. We can probe further to discover what we missed, fall back to an alternate advance, or both depending on the circumstances.

This subtle yet very important difference between question one of The Perfect Close and other closing techniques is a critical nuance that you need to get right when phrasing this question. Or, you may get it wrong and not achieve the outcome you were hoping for.

Getting it Wrong

Toward the end of a frenetic quarter, a young, new member of my team contacted me regarding an opportunity he hoped to close by the end of the quarter. He reported that his prospect had a proposal and had been through all the steps of our selling process. So, it seemed like everything was in line for an end-of-quarter close. To seal the deal, my rep sought approval on a concession he hoped to offer his prospect as an incentive to get them to buy before the end of the quarter.

I prefer to avoid offering concessions to accelerate timing, but since all of the preliminaries seemed to have been completed, I directed him to use one of the classic applications of The Perfect Close which I call Something Special. I told him to ask, "*Does it make sense* for me to see if we can do something special for you if we can get everything wrapped up by the end of the quarter?"

Curious, my rep asked, "Well, what if he says yes? What is the special something that we might do for them?"

"We have lots of options depending on what they might value the most. Let's just see if the timing works."

Persistently my rep asked for more clarification, "Well what kinds of things are possible?"

"There are all kinds of things. We could adjust the terms, the deposit, we could change the licensing scope, tweak the maintenance; we could get them some user-group passes. There are a lot of directions we can take it."

"Can we get them a discount?"

"Sure. Discounting is one of the options. Let's just start with the timing, and then as a second step we can determine which concession will be most effective."

"Okay. I'll call them right now. Thanks!"

A little while later I saw my rep in the hall looking disappointed. I inquired how the call had gone with his opportunity, and he replied, "Your question didn't work at all."

"Oh really? What happened?"

"Well, I asked him your question, and he got all angry and then asked me to create a new proposal with a bigger discount on it."

"Really. That's surprising. Why did he get angry?"

"He said he would let me know when he was ready to buy, and he was mad that we hadn't already offered him our best price."

"So, he immediately assumed that 'something special' meant a discount? That's strange."

"Yep. Now I have to create a new proposal," whined my rep.

Coincidentally, we were testing a new phone system that would let us audit calls for coaching purposes, so I decided to review the call myself. Here's what I found:

Instead of asking, "*Does it makes sense* for me to see if we can do something special for you if we can get everything wrapped up by the end of the quarter?" my rep said, "If you will sign before the end of the quarter, I can get you a bigger discount."

This is wholly different than what I instructed him to say. In effect, "Will you sign before the end of the quarter if I give you a discount?" makes the question about the action rather than about the timing. He was asking, "Will you or won't you do X?"

As I continued listening through the conversation I heard the client say something very interesting. He said, "I haven't even run the proposal I have now – which was supposed to be your final proposal – past our board yet, and they don't meet until the 15th of next month."

By rephrasing the question, my rep put his prospect in a difficult, perhaps impossible, situation (to convene the board within two days for an impromptu, emergency approval) which clearly made him angry. This guy clearly wanted our solution. It was just a question of timing.

My rep also replaced "something special" with "discount." Concessions are best left undefined until we know the timing is right. Once we know that closing is possible, then we can determine what concession will have the greatest impact.

While coaching my rep afterwards, I told him I was curious why he had changed the question so dramatically even after he had written it down. His reply was that he understood the concept and didn't reference his notes at all during the call. He thought he was speeding things up by changing what was going to be a two-step process (ask about timing, then discuss "something special") down to a single question, "Will you buy if I give you a discount?"

Next, I asked why he went straight for "discount" instead of "something special." Again, he felt he was upgrading the question and speeding things up by deciding in advance that a discount was the best of the options.

This was an eye-opening experience for my rep that taught him the importance of following the nuance prescribed in The Perfect Close. He learned to apply it regularly and went on to become one of my best users of the approach.

So, what can we learn about The Perfect Close from this experience?
1. Asking about the timing of a possible action is different than asking for that action. It elicits a different response, and it feels emotionally different.
2. The Perfect Close is a two question, two-step process. Sometimes you will only need to use the first question. Trying to shortcut the process typically backfires. At the very least it reintroduces all of the risks of a direct close and eliminates all the benefits of The Perfect Close. Be patient. Your client WILL let you ask your second question. They are not going to suddenly stop talking to you mid-conversation.
3. Stick to the recommended phrasing. There is plenty of room in The Perfect Close to tailor it to your individual style. However, first have a clear understanding of how your changes will affect your client's reactions. Until you have mastered this, stick to the recommended phrasing.

What happened to my young rep's deal? We ultimately won the opportunity about a month later when our contact was able to get board approval on our final proposal, which had been discounted (as my rep had suggested was available).

There are a couple other bonus learning moments we can draw from this experience:
1. Timing issues are not price issues. With this deal it was never about the price or additional concessions. It was about timing. Our contact was sold with the original offer and was moving it through his internal timeline. Operating in sync with the buyer's buying process would have brought the opportunity in at higher margin.
2. Telegraphing a concession means giving that concession. Once a client hears a concession is possible, count on giving it. By changing "something special" to "discount," my rep had ultimately committed to giving a discount. In the Something Special application of The Perfect Close, it's important that we enter the conversation without a particular concession in mind. Your attitude should be, "I don't know what my options are without talking to some folks, but if the timing is right I'll go see what I can do." We will further discuss the "Something Special" application later in the chapter, but you'll find that Something Special accomplishes three important things: a) it doesn't telegraph any specific concession; b) it answers the timing question of what is possible; c) it positions you as an advocate for the client.

 **CLOSING SECRET** - Timing issues are not price issues.

How to Get it Right

The rest of this chapter will be about getting it right. One of the beautiful things about The Perfect Close is that you don't have to understand it for it to work. It just works. Even if you don't know why. So, learn the basics, use the recommended phrases and when you have mastered the psychology, tailor it and make it your own.

EXERCISE #40 - The Perfect Close Question One

Instructions: Using the advances you created in on page 69 Exercise #24 - Brainstorming Advances, select appropriate ideal and alternate advances for your next few appointments and create your own Perfect Close Question One. Write the exact phrases below.

Appointment #1:
Ideal Advance
Alternative Advance 1
Alternative Advance 2
Appointment #2:
Ideal Advance
Alternative Advance 1
Alternative Advance 2
Appointment #3:
Ideal Advance
Alternative Advance 1
Alternative Advance 2
Appointment #4:
Ideal Advance
Alternative Advance 1
Alternative Advance 2
Appointment #5:
Ideal Advance
Alternative Advance 1
Alternative Advance 2

Group Exercise: In groups less than 20, go around the room and have each member vocalize their Perfect Close Question for their first appointment. Time permitting, repeat the process with your additional appointments. In groups larger than 20 pair up with a partner and take turns practicing all five of your Perfect Close questions on each other.

There are only two possible outcomes of the first Perfect Close question, "Does it make sense to X?" Yes or no. If "Yes," then you just successfully executed The Perfect Close and got your advance with a single question! It's time to schedule that next step (because we know the timing is right, right?).

But... what if they say, "No"?

If They Say No

"No, it doesn't make sense to talk about doing X?" Now what?

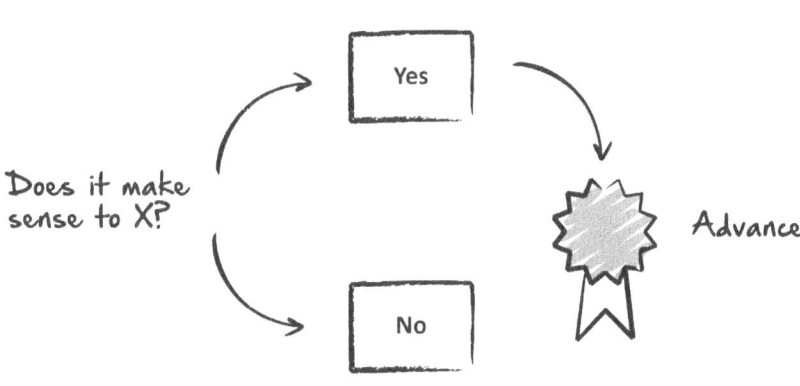

Did they say, "No, I will not buy?" Did they say, "No, I will not take your action?" When our client answers, "no" to the question, "Does it make sense?" they are simply saying that the timing is not yet right for that step. This is perfectly okay because each client's process has its own unique dynamics that affect the speed and timing. So, if your suggested advance was reasonable and logical, you're probably wondering, "Hmm... I guess they're not where I thought they were. So, what does make sense right now?"

> When a client answers, "no" to question one, they are simply saying that the timing is not yet right for that step.

This is the key attitude to have with question two of The Perfect Close – figuring out what does make sense right now.

Question Two of The Perfect Close

The basic response to hearing, "no" to question one is, "Okay. What is a good next step then?"

> Question two of the perfect close is:
> "What is a good next step then?"

After years of using this approach and teaching it to others I can tell you what happens in 90% of cases – your client will simply suggest a very logical next step for advancing the sale.

I cannot overstate the impact of this. We don't have to be clairvoyant or a mastermind of the buyer's journey. In fact, we could be brand new to selling without the tiniest clue of what ought to happen next, and it will still work because the customer is suggesting it for us. This makes it perfect for both inexperienced and seasoned professionals.

🗝️ **CLOSING SECRET** - Clients will always be comfortable with their own suggested next steps.

🗝 **CLOSING SECRET** - In the beginning we are all inexperienced.

As a manager, I hire individuals with some sales experience, but they generally have no experience with the solutions we offer nor all the possible dimensions that our clients go through in their buying process. Should I wait until my new hire has mastered all things before placing them into the field? With complex solutions, that could be a very long time indeed.

What about professionals starting a new venture? They might be experts in their field but have no experience with selling. Should they master selling before embarking in their given profession?

Nope. New sellers or inexperienced professionals can become productive almost immediately without any concern that they will come off as pushy. The Perfect Close is perfect for them. If they miss the mark on question one, the customer will guide them through the next logical step when they answer question number two.

🗝 **CLOSING SECRET** - The Perfect Close allows inexperienced professionals to be productive immediately.

Example Vignettes of The Perfect Close

Sound too easy? These vignettes illustrate just how simple it is.

PROFESSIONAL: "Well, Jeff, now that you've seen a full demonstration it's pretty common to want to see it humming in a live environment at a client site. Does it make sense for us to talk about scheduling a site visit for you?

CLIENT: "No, I don't think we need that yet."

PROFESSIONAL: "Gotcha. Well what do you think would make a good next step then?"

CLIENT: "Well, there are some other people here that I think would benefit from seeing this. Would it be okay if we scheduled another demonstration for them?"

PROFESSIONAL: "Sure. Let's look at some dates together."

PROFESSIONAL: "Does it make sense for us to talk about putting together a financial assessment of your current situation to see where and what the upside might be?"

CLIENT: "No, I don't think so."

PROFESSIONAL: "I see. Well what do you think would make a good next step then?"

CLIENT: "The assessment sounds valuable. Do you have an example of something you've prepared for another client, so we can review it as a team?"

PROFESSIONAL: "Absolutely. Let's schedule some time to go over it together so you know what you're looking at, and then you can explain it to your team. Or, I'd be happy to do that for you, if you like."

PROFESSIONAL: "Does it make sense for us to talk about getting your credit approved while we go through the other details together?"

CLIENT: "Not at all. You're way ahead of yourself here."

PROFESSIONAL: "Okay. What do you see as a good next step then?"

CLIENT: "I'm going to need to see a complete statement of work for the whole project before we do anything like that."

PROFESSIONAL: "Of course, that makes great sense. Let me put that together, and let's schedule a time to go over it to make sure we have everything right."

The Softening Statement

There's one nuance of question two that I call The Softening Statement. After the potential client communicates that the timing isn't right, did you notice in each example that our professional immediately follows with a brief understanding statement? There are wide variety of possible softening statements. Here are a few examples:

- Got it.
- Gotcha.
- Okay.
- I see.
- I understand.
- Mmmm...
- All right.
- Oh, okay.
- I'm tracking.
- Sounds like I missed the mark.
- Sounds like the timing isn't right for that yet.
- Let's stay in sync then.
- Let's move at your pace then.

Practice them a few times to find what works for you. I prefer the shorter ones. Sometimes, when understanding and rapport is already present, it isn't necessary to state it as it's conveyed in your eyes, a nod, or another understanding gesture.

These statements or actions acknowledge that you heard them, that you understand them, and that they're in control. It also naturally flows into question two, "What is a good next step then?"

As previously noted, intent matters more than technique. So, if you have conveyed good intent, don't get hung up on the technique. Do what's natural for you, then ask for a good next step.

The formula for question two of The Perfect Close looks like:

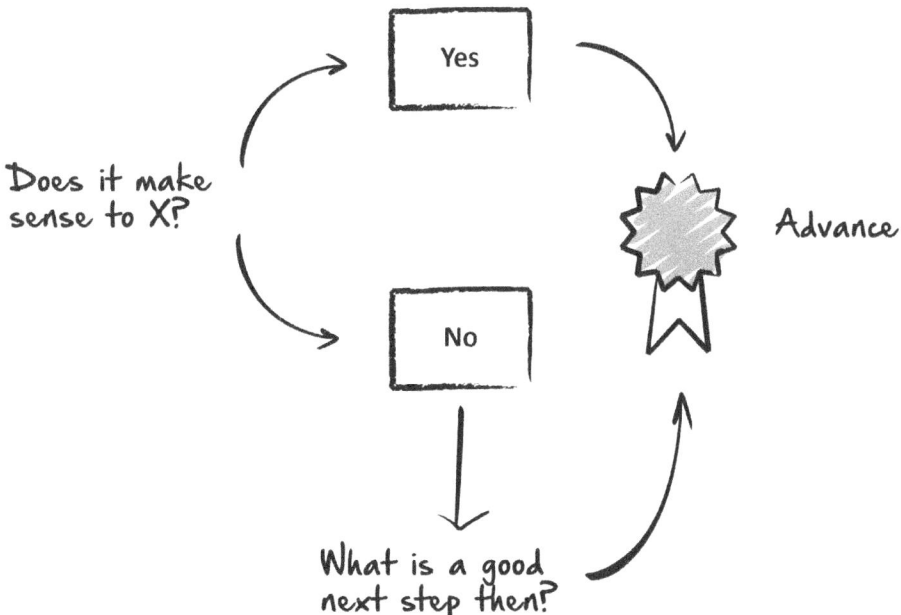

Here we see The Perfect Close model with both questions incorporated showing how The Perfect Close produces an advance. If you are with a genuine prospect, this simple model will produce a successful advance 90-95% of the time. Try it yourself and keep track. I would love to hear about your experiences at PureMuir.com.

# EXERCISE #41 - The Perfect Close Question Two

Instructions: Refer back to the advances you compiled on page 126 with Exercise #40. Then, pair up with a partner to role play the following sequence:

Sales Professional: Ask for your Ideal Advance using The Perfect Close phrase you created.

Client: Decline.

Sales Professional: Use a softening statement then ask question two of The Perfect Close (some variation of "What is a good next step?")

Client: Offer a logical next step.

Switch roles and repeat.

Variations to Improve Your Success

95% is excellent, but I have to admit, it's not perfect. These variations of The Perfect Close will help you shore up that final 5%.

The Suggestion

This minor tweak is especially helpful when your prospect doesn't have much purchasing experience and doesn't know how to go about evaluating options. They need you to navigate for them, and this method will help you shorten their sales cycle. It requires that you have a clear understanding of the most common or logical steps that prospects go through when purchasing your product or service because you are going to suggest that path with each advance (the topic we covered in Chapter 9 - What Do I Want My Prospective Client to Do?).

Simply add one additional statement before asking question number one:

> "Other clients at this stage typically take X as a next step in their evaluation."

Here, X is your ideal advance. For example:

> "Other clients at this stage typically schedule a meeting between us and your team so we can get their input and participation on what would help them the most. Does it make sense for us to schedule a meeting with your team, so we can get their input on what would be most beneficial for them?"

A couple more examples:

"Other clients at this stage typically schedule time to watch a procedure where the device is utilized, and then have a follow-up discussion with the surgical team. Does it make sense for us to talk about scheduling a time for you to see the procedure at a client site?"

"Other clients at this stage typically have us perform a workflow analysis so we can see where you'll get the most improvement. Does it make sense for us to talk about scheduling a workflow analysis, so we can see where the best efficiencies can be gained?"

Using this variation, you walk your client through each stage of the process.

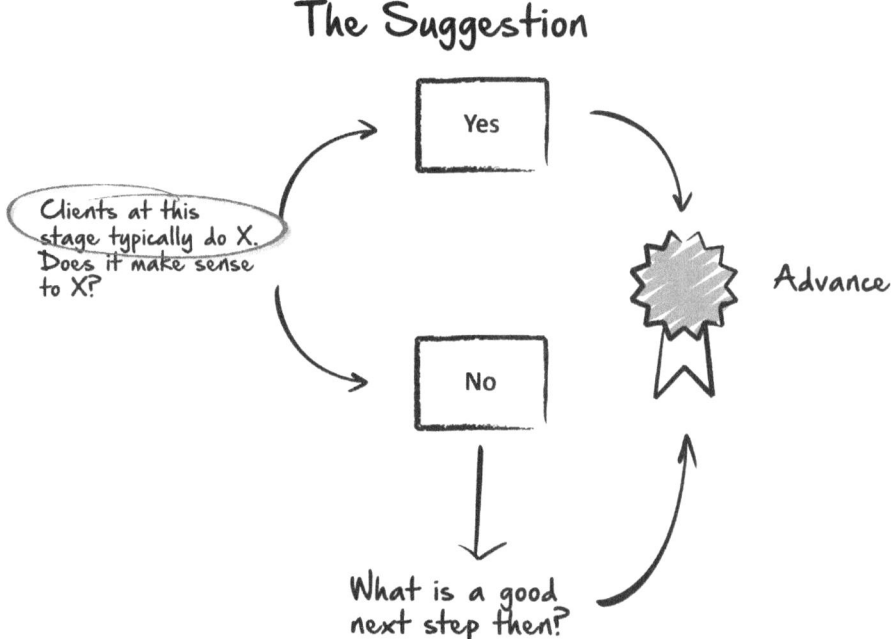

Yet (and this is an important distinction), you are still asking and advancing at a comfortable pace for your prospect which generates a ton of value for unsure buyers and, perhaps, a lot of gratitude.

One final comment. Consider mapping all of the common steps at this juncture. Then, the path will be clear to both of you, and, if they agree, you can simply help your client through each step.

 ### EXERCISE #42 - "The Suggestion"

Instructions: Using the same appointments and advances in Exercise #40, pair up with a partner to practice using the Suggestion model for your ideal advances. One plays the client and the other plays the sales professional. If needed, write out the exact Perfect Close Phrase you will use for your Advances using "The Suggestion" model.

Take turns switching roles and your Perfect Close phrases with "The Suggestion" model incorporated.

The Fall-Back

It's important that you learn this variation since you will use it anytime you are unable to get your ideal advance and you fall back to a secondary or back-up advance. It usually requires a suggestion component, as in the example above, so a good understanding of the typical buying process your clients go through is beneficial. This is why we did the advances exercises earlier.

It looks like this:

Question 1: "Does it makes sense to do X?"
Question 2 (if question one fails): "Clients at this stage typically do X. Does it make sense to do X?"
Question 3 (if question two fails): "What's a good next step then?"

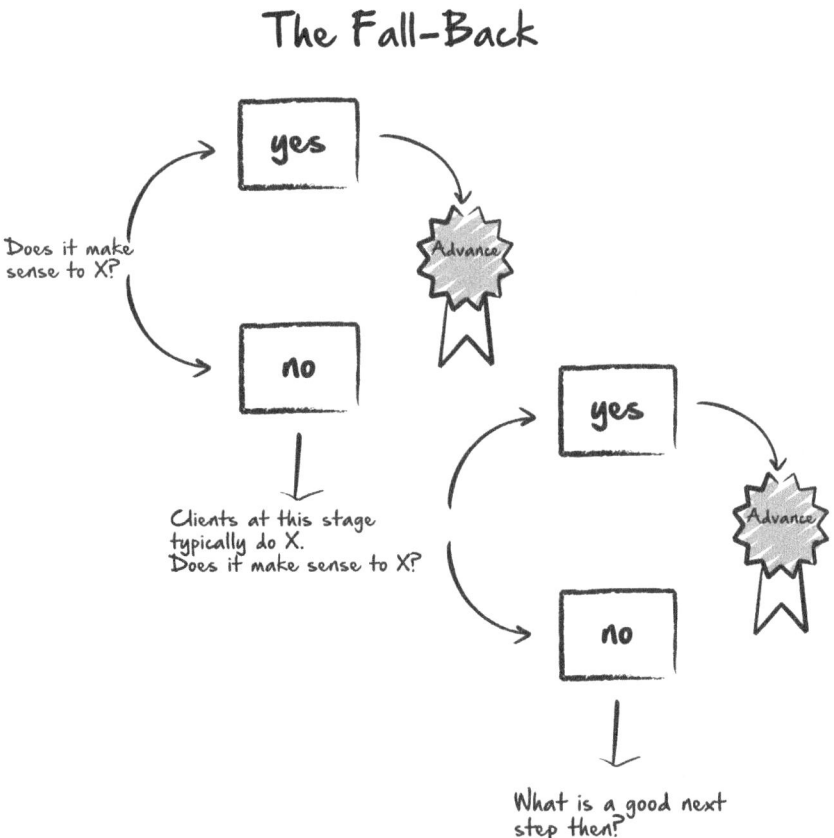

Examples:

PROFESSIONAL: "Nathan, does it make sense for us to talk about doing a workflow analysis, so we can see where the best efficiencies can be gained?"

CLIENT: "Mmm… I don't think so."

PROFESSIONAL: "Okay. A lot of folks at this stage will schedule a demonstration for their whole team to get their reaction and feedback. Does it make sense for us to schedule a demonstration for your whole team, so they can see it in action?"

CLIENT: "That's just what I was thinking."

PROFESSIONAL: "Isaac, does it make sense for us to talk about getting your credit approved while we go through the other details together?"

CLIENT: "Oooh… I don't know," (body language says he's clearly uncomfortable).

PROFESSIONAL: "All right. Well, most clients at this stage will complete the financial goals part of the plan, and then schedule a time for us to go over it together and talk through some options. Does it make sense for us to schedule that?"

CLIENT: "That would be perfect. Then, I can go over it with Terri before we meet again."

PROFESSIONAL: "Hey, Kelly, does it make sense for us to schedule some time for our technical teams to get together so we can get a clearer picture of the requirements?"

CLIENT: "Mmm… I don't think so."

PROFESSIONAL: "Gotcha. Most clients at this stage will have us do a site assessment so we can see what we can leverage from your existing infrastructure. Does it make sense for us to schedule a time to come do a site assessment for you?"

CLIENT: "I don't know about that…"

PROFESSIONAL: "I see. What would you say is a good next step then?"

CLIENT: "What I'd like to do is have you meet our CIO first. Would that be okay?"

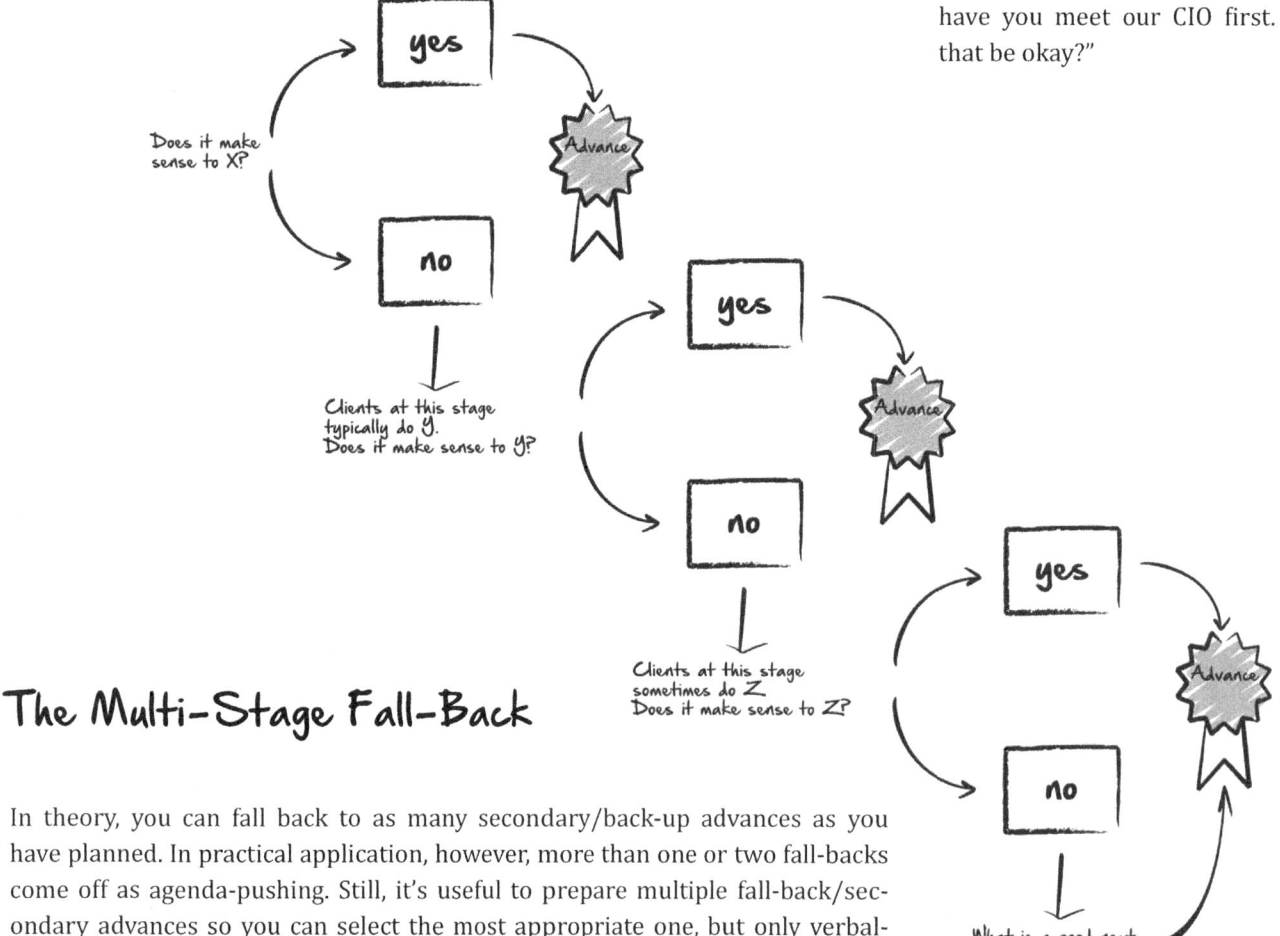

The Multi-Stage Fall-Back

In theory, you can fall back to as many secondary/back-up advances as you have planned. In practical application, however, more than one or two fall-backs come off as agenda-pushing. Still, it's useful to prepare multiple fall-back/secondary advances so you can select the most appropriate one, but only verbalize one or two.

 **EXERCISE #43** - "The Fall-Back"

Instructions: Using the same appointments and advances from Exercise #40, pair up with a partner. One plays the client and the other plays the sales professional. You shouldn't need to write out anything new. Only the timing and presentation of your alternative fall-back advances is changed in this exercise.

Take turns switching roles and practicing your Perfect Close phrases with "The Suggestion" model incorporated with "The Fall-Back" model using the following format:

Sales Professional: Ask for your Ideal Advance using The Perfect Close phrase you created. (Use "The Suggestion" as part of this for bonus points.)

Client: Decline.

Sales Professional: Use a softening statement then present the first of your alternative fall-back advances.

Client: Decline.

Sales Professional: Use a softening statement then present the second of your alternative fall-back advances.

Client: Decline.

Sales Professional: Use a softening statement then ask question two of The Perfect Close (some variation of "What do you think is a good next step?")

Client: Offer a logical next step.

The Add-On

With this variation instead of falling back to your alternate advances, you add them on after achieving your ideal advance. Like the previous variations, it usually requires a suggestion component so a good understanding of the typical buying process your clients go through is beneficial since all we're doing is matching your sales cycle with their buying cycle. So, if the client is ready to move at a faster pace, we can keep up by incrementally adding advances.

The only distinction between the Add-On and the Fall-Back is ending with "Are there any other logical steps we should be taking right now?" rather than, "What is a good next step then?" This gives the buyer a chance to suggest logical action steps that we may not have considered.

Here is what the model looks like:

Question 1: "Does it makes sense to do X?"
Question 2 (after question one succeeds): "Clients at this stage very often also do Y. Does it make sense to do Y?"
Question 3 (after question two also succeeds): "We can also do Z if it makes sense. Does it make sense to do Z?"
Question 4 (if question three fails): "Okay. Are there any other logical steps we should be taking right now?"

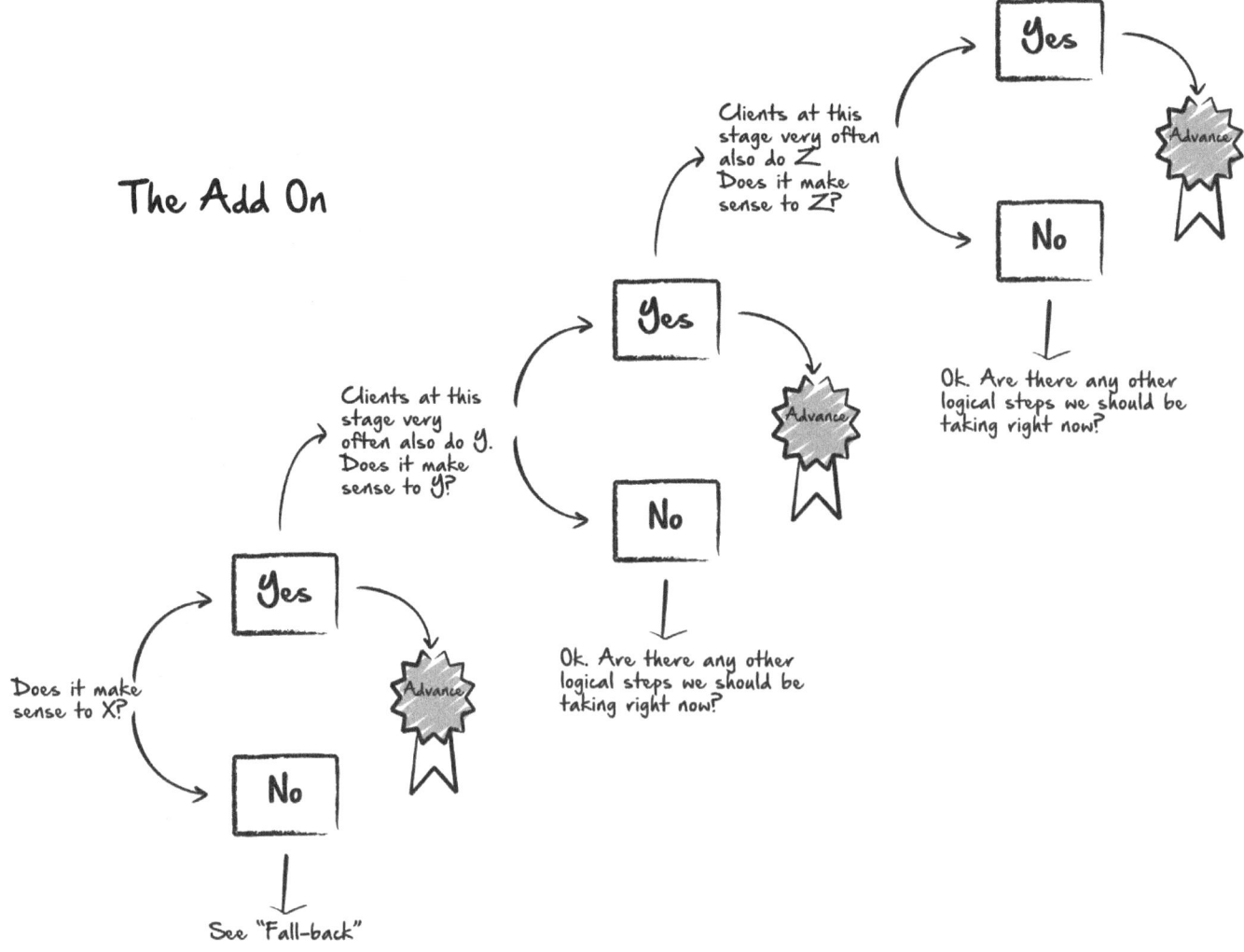

Examples:

PROFESSIONAL: "Hey, Don, does it make sense for us to talk about putting together a financial assessment of your current situation?"

CLIENT: "Oh yes. We need to see that."

PROFESSIONAL: "Great. I'll schedule that with your team. A lot of clients at this stage will also have us present those results to their board. Does it make sense for us to schedule a time to present the results?"

CLIENT: "Yeah, that would be extremely helpful. The best time would be two weeks from now at our board meeting. Is that too soon?"

PROFESSIONAL: "Let's plan for it, and we'll burn the midnight oil so we can make your meeting. Some groups want to see our HQ where all the magic happens. Do you have any interest in visiting the HQ?"

CLIENT: "Nah, that isn't necessary."

PROFESSIONAL: "Got it. Are there any other logical steps we should be taking right now?"

CLIENT: "I know Chris is going to want to see references. Can you get me a list of clients he can call if he wants?"

PROFESSIONAL: "Absolutely. I'll put everything together for us."

PROFESSIONAL: "Hey, Regan, does it make sense for us to talk about scheduling a demo for the rest of your team so we can get their input and participation?"

CLIENT: "Yes. We need everyone on board."

PROFESSIONAL: "Great. Let's look at some possible dates. A lot of clients at this stage will also have us schedule time for both our technical teams to discuss the dynamics around the conversion. Does it make sense for us to schedule our tech people to meet?"

CLIENT: "Absolutely. My guys are worried about that. That's a great idea."

PROFESSIONAL: "Okay. I'll get some dates, and we can coordinate. I think we have everything we need for a proposal. Does it make sense for me to put together a preliminary proposal so you can get a feel for the scope of the project?"

CLIENT: "Yes. That would be really helpful."

PROFESSIONAL: "Okay. I've got some homework here. Are there any other logical steps we should be taking right now?"

CLIENT: "Well, is there any chance I can see a copy of your standard agreement? Our legal team can be kind of slow sometimes."

PROFESSIONAL: "Absolutely. I know what you're talking about. I'll get you a copy of that so your legal team can start reviewing it."

Unlike the Fall-Back variation, there doesn't seem to be a point of diminishing returns for Add-Ons. The second example is an excerpt of an actual, real-life conversation. My team and I never dreamed that sending an agreement would emerge as a realistic next step. In fact, it's possible that had we suggested sending a contract as our first ideal advance Regan (not the client's real name) would've been put off. Instead, by diplomatically pacing it at the buyer's rate, we scored an amazing four advances (one of which we hadn't even thought of ourselves)!

Obviously, this is the best and most fun of all the variations because we just keep piling on advances until we've met their pace and with each one, the sales cycle hastens.

EXERCISE #44 - "The Add-On"

Instructions: Continuing with the same appointments and advances from Exercise #40, pair up with a partner to practice using The Add-On model. One plays the client and the other plays the sales professional. If needed, write out the exact Perfect Close Phrases you will use for your Advances.

Take turns switching roles and practicing your Perfect Close phrases with "The Add-On" model incorporated using the following format:

Sales Professional: Ask for your Ideal Advance using The Perfect Close phrase you created. (Use "The Suggestion" as part of this for bonus points.)

Client: Accept.

Sales Professional: Use a softening statement then present the first of your alternative Add-on advances.

Client: Accept.

Sales Professional: Use a softening statement then present the second of your alternative Add-on advances.

Client: Accept.

Sales Professional: Use a softening statement then ask the final question of the Add-on model (some variation of "Are there any other logical steps we should be considering?")

Client: Offer a logical next step.

The Reverse Order

This final variation is the most open but comes with caveats. In this model you reverse The Perfect Close questions and ask question two before question one. It looks like this:

Question 1: "What would you say is a good next step?"
Question 2 (if the client is stumped): "Does it make sense for us to X?"'

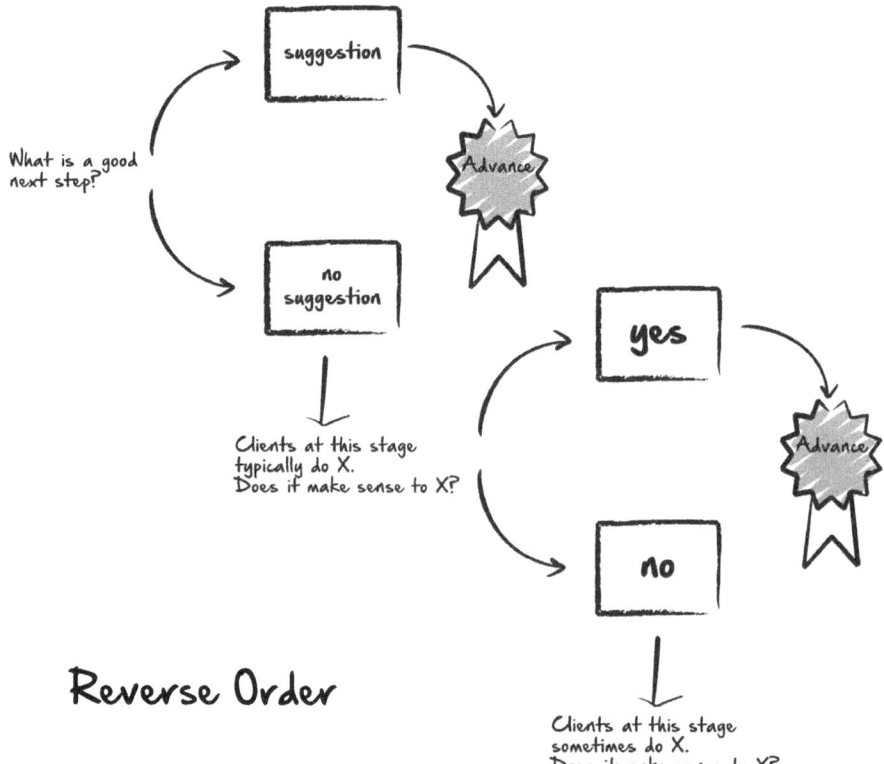

Reverse Order

Examples:

PROFESSIONAL: "Well, Mike, what would you say is a good next step?"
CLIENT: "I was thinking it would be helpful to talk to an existing client here in Australia."
PROFESSIONAL: "No problem. I'll set it up for us. Let's look at your calendar."

PROFESSIONAL: "So, Mike, what would you say is a good next step?"
CLIENT: "Uh, nothing comes to mind really."
PROFESSIONAL: "Well, other clients at this stage typically want to see it live in operation. Does it make sense for us to talk about getting you out to a client site?"

This variation has advantages as well as drawbacks. Use this less-assertive model if:

a. You have not yet learned your clientele's typical buying process, and you're unsure what an appropriate next step might be. Because it is wide open, it offers more possibilities than you might have considered with your own suggested advances – which could be good or bad since a client-suggested advance isn't necessarily the best advance for them or for you. The biggest drawback is that the buyer may not be able to come up with a good next step (or any next step, which is always possible), but usually, they will suggest an appropriate step which will ultimately teach you something about your clientele's buying process. Regardless, invest time to learn that information so you can use the other models.

b. You have a strong-willed individual who clearly knows what they want and likes to be in the driver's seat (or if context dictates that you are as open as possible in order to maintain rapport). While most buyers appreciate helpful facilitation, a small percentage can be put off by the slightest assertion, so when it's important that the buyer feels in control of the process, use this model.

EXERCISE #46 - "The Reverse Order"

Instructions: Again, continuing with the same appointments and advances used in Exercises #40, pair up with a partner to practice The Reverse Order model. One plays the client and the other plays the sales professional. If needed, write out the exact Perfect Close Phrase you will use for your Advances using "The Reverse Order" model.

Take turns switching roles and practicing your Perfect Close phrases with "The Reverse Order" model incorporated using the following format:

Round 1

   Sales Professional: Ask some variation of "What do you think is a good next step?"

   Client: Suggest a logical next step.

Round 2

   Sales Professional: Ask some variation of "What do you think is a good next step?"

   Client: Act stumped.

   Sales Professional: Use the Suggestion Model of The Perfect Close phrase you created for your Ideal Advance.

   Client: Accept.

   Sales Professional: [Optional] Use the "Add-on" model to suggest either of your alternate add-on advances.

Remember to switch roles so that both parties get to practice both rounds.

Classic Application of The Perfect Close – Something Special

There are unlimited usage possibilities of The Perfect Close, but the application used far more frequently than others is Something Special, and it works perfectly for accelerated closings and upselling situations.

Every salesperson is familiar with the pressures surrounding end-of-period quotas. Unfortunately, these pressures give rise to many dysfunctional selling practices. One common tactic is to offer concessions in order to close sales before the end of a given time.

I don't like giving concessions – especially, to buy business. My experience is that at the final stage of most complex sales, you have less than 10–15% control over the timing of when a deal will close. Sales cycles can definitely be shortened, but the shortening happens earlier in the cycle not at the end.

Nevertheless, a common mistake that inexperienced professionals make is to offer a discount or some incentive to induce their buyer to close sooner. The main problem with this is that clients tend to ignore the timing requirement and see the concession as an indicator of what the offer should have been all along. Then, they expect these concessions regardless of when they close, whether it is in your desired time frame or not. Once you offer a concession, your client is expecting that concession regardless of all other factors.

These discounts trade margin for timing. As previously mentioned, I don't advocate discounting to accelerate timing. However, having worked for a publicly traded company for almost two decades, I do understand the dynamics involved as revenue recognized in this quarter may have more value to the company than in the following quarter. So, I have some history with executive management encouraging accelerated end-of-quarter sales , often by whatever means possible.

I recall a particular situation where I had exactly ten new-business opportunities in play. One was ripe and ready to close, but the others were somewhere in the middle of their buying process. Two weeks before quarter's end we received word from above – use all legal means to close business.

To induce an accelerated close, I offered discounts to all ten accounts with the condition that signed agreements would be received by the end of that month.

One deal signed. The very one that was already at the closing stage. The remaining nine chose to continue their evaluation rather than take advantage of the discounts. Naturally, I continued working these into the subsequent quarter, and ultimately we closed seven more of the original ten for a total of eight.

Unfortunately, on every opportunity there was an awkward conversation about whether or not they could get the same discount I offered the previous quarter. "If it was worth it to you before, why isn't it worth it to you now?" they would ask. Avoiding or denying their request sometimes created a tangible erosion of goodwill. Ironically, as the new quarter approached its end, I found myself in the same fire drill. Of course, I used the opportunity to offer the discounts they expected, and all ended well – albeit with lower margins as I had unintentionally trained my buyers to wait for the end of the quarter to get concessions.

This dynamic caused me to think creatively about how to offer concessions. And thus, Something Special was born.

Applying Something Special

Many professionals have told me that this one close is among the most valuable things they've ever learned in sales. You be the judge. Here it is, verbatim:

"Does it make sense for me to see if we can do something special for you if we can get everything wrapped up by the end of the quarter?"

Naturally, use whatever timeframe suits your situation.

As mentioned earlier in Getting It Wrong, enter the conversation without any particular concession in mind. Determining what is special to the client requires another step and further conversation. Your mindset should be, "I don't know what my options are yet, but if wrapping things up is a possibility, I'll see what I can do."

The beauty is that if the timing isn't right for the client, you won't have to get approval for "something special" and your margins are preserved going into the next period. However, if the buyer says it is possible to wrap things up, you have a two options:

1. Ask what they find most valuable. Without guaranteeing anything, let them give you a "something special" list.
2. Tell them you'll see what you can do and report back. Then, discuss your options with your manager.

Usually, you'll use both options together. If you suspect the client will suggest concessions you know you can't satisfy, skip option one. Concessions vary by industry, but common ones involve delivery, training, additional services, optional modules, maintenance, payment options, etc. Often my client's preference for a concession is not what I was expecting – frequently valuing services over price discounts. Knowing their preferences gives you flexibility in crafting your offer, and if a client values something that costs your company less, it's a real win-win.

Examples:

PROFESSIONAL: "Gary, does it make sense for me to see if we can do something special for you if we can get everything wrapped up by the end of the month?"

CLIENT: "I'd love that, but our CEO is out until after the holidays. I can't do anything until he's back." (Margin Preserved)

PROFESSIONAL: "Hey, Gary, does it make sense for me to see if we can do something special for you if we can get everything wrapped up by the end of the week?"

CLIENT: "Maybe. What did you have in mind?"

PROFESSIONAL: "Well, I don't know what my options are without talking to some folks, but if the timing is right I'll go see what I can do."

CLIENT: "If the offer is right, I think we can do something. Go find out what you can do."

PROFESSIONAL: "Hey, Gary, does it make sense for me to see if we can do something special for you if we wrap things up by the end of the quarter?"

CLIENT: "Like what?"

PROFESSIONAL: "I don't know without talking to our CEO, but if we can do something this quarter he said he's willing to work with clients."

CLIENT: "If the offer's good, we're ready. Let's find out what he's thinking."

PROFESSIONAL: "You got it. To speed things up, are there areas in the proposal where you need to add value? If so, maybe it's something we can consider."

CLIENT: "Michelle is concerned that some staff will need more training than usual. Anything you can do in that area will make me a hero with her. From my perspective, it would also be great if you could do something with the maintenance. Lowering it or starting it later would be great. That's it, maintenance and training."

Does it make sense for me to see if we can do something special for you if we can get everything wrapped up by …?

Something Special accomplishes three important things:

1. It doesn't telegraph any kind of concession or the size of that concession.
2. It reveals whether the client is nearly ready to close and able to do it within your suggested timeframe.
3. It positions you as their advocate for the client since you are doing this on their behalf.

If you've ever found yourself on the end-of-quarter discount rollercoaster, you will appreciate how Something Special preserves both revenues and your commissions.

EXERCISE #47 - Something Special

Instructions: Pair up with a partner. One plays the client and the other plays the sales professional. Take turns switching roles and practicing the "Something Special" variation of The Perfect Close using the conversational guideline below. Initially, practice it verbatim. Prepare yourself for the questions that typically follow the "Something Special" model.

Round 1

Sales Professional: "Does it make sense for me to see if we can do something special for you if we can get everything wrapped up by the end of the quarter?"

Client: Respond in the negative and describe why the timing doesn't work.

Round 2

Sales Professional: "Does it make sense for me to see if we can do something special for you if we can get everything wrapped up by the end of the quarter?"

Client: Respond with curiosity and ask what the something special is in some way.

Sales Professional: Say you are uncertain but if timing is right you'll see what you can do.

Client: Respond that if the offer is good enough the timing is possible.

Sales Professional: Confirm that you will be their advocate and then ask what type of concession they would value most (but don't promise that concession). Talk through the concession as needed and then confirm that you will go see what you can do.

Remember to switch roles so that both parties get to practice both rounds.

EXERCISE #48 - Perfect Close Group Discussion

Instructions: Break into groups of 3-4 and discuss your experience role-playing your use of The Perfect Close. Review the following questions together:

- How does The Perfect Close make you feel when using it? Is it comfortable to use?
- How did you feel when you were playing the client? Did you feel pressured?
- How can you see yourself applying The Perfect Close in your type of sale?
- What kind of outcome do you expect you will receive by using it?
- What do you feel are the keys to making The Perfect Close successful?
- What is the greatest insight you received as part of the exercise?

Group Discussion: Each of the group writes their greatest insight on a flipchart or whiteboard and then each group shares their list of top insights with the rest of the group.

Best Practice Principles for Using The Perfect Close

By now, you should have a clear understanding of the model and just how simple it is. Many individuals have learned the model in less time than it took you to go through this chapter. Let's wrap up this section by discussing how to best use The Perfect Close in your daily selling and business development activities.

- Initially, you'll get the best results by using the suggested phrasing. Before you tailor it to your individual style, have a clear understanding of how, and why, your changes might affect your client's reactions. Once you have a solid foundation of success with The Perfect Close works, a whole world of possible variations will open up to you, and I'd love to hear about them at PureMuir.com.
- Know your clientele's typical buying process, but The Perfect Close will work even if you aren't completely sure of your prospect's buying process. However, the more you know about the buying process, the more you can help them by suggesting logical and productive advances that will eventually reach the outcomes they seek.
- Good selling depends on good planning more than any other single factor. Prepare an ideal advance and several alternative or backup advances before every sales encounter. This assures you the ability and flexibility to utilize the Fall-Back and Add-On variations of The Perfect Close and match your sales efforts with your prospect's pace.
- Use The Perfect Close in every sales encounter to advance your opportunity in some way. It's a risk-free way of testing and then asking for an advance. There is no downside to using it every time. Doing so, you'll quickly master The Perfect Close and improve your closing ratio. Like diets, the most successful closing regimen is the one you can stick to. Instead of learning a different close for each situation, master one close for all situations.
- Use the Fall-Back variation every time your client responds that your ideal advance doesn't make sense and increase the chances that a productive advance will be the outcome of your meeting. You can still end with, "What's a good next step then?"
- Use the Add-On variation every time your client accepts your ideal advance, then make sure you're moving at the right pace by asking if it makes sense for them to consider one of your alternate advances. Again, since using The Perfect Close is risk free, you may potentially accelerate the pace without adding tension or appearing pushy.

Conclusion

Congratulations! You just learned The Perfect Close. The Perfect Close has made a tremendous difference in my life and the lives of many others. It's so simple, but mastery requires repetition, and you won't find a better payoff for your time. With a little practice you'll become proficient in less time than it took you to go through this chapter.

If you skipped right to this chapter to jumpstart your closing skills, I encourage you to now complete the rest of the book so you can experience maximum benefit. Combining what you have learned in this chapter with the principles covered in previous chapters will shorten your sales cycle, maximize the impact of each meeting, and advance your sales in a way that differentiates you from your competition.

Illustrations of The Perfect Close models can help accelerate your understanding and mastery of the approach. Download a copy of The Perfect Close Model at PureMuir.com/TPCworkbook.

In the next chapter we'll pull it all together in one clear picture so your handle on The Perfect Close is complete.

CHAPTER 14

Putting It All Together

"A set of organized steps that align with the buyer's buying process will help a sales professional become more engaged in that process, more aware of the buyer's actions, and better informed as to your opportunity to close the sale."

– Michael Nick

Now, let's put together everything you've learned into seven simple steps. Use this section as a checklist for your next sales encounter.

Get out your forms or a blank sheet of paper and a pen because it's time to commit your plan to paper.

Here are the seven steps:

1. Research Your Client
2. Determine Your Value Proposition
3. Define Your Questions
4. Determine Your Advances
5. Define Your Unexpected Value
6. Create Your Agenda
7. Prepare Your Mindset

STEP 1 - Research Your Client

Use the questions and forms in Chapter 11 to research your client. This helps us better understand the client's situation, determine what we know and don't know, and how we might best create value for this client.

STEP 2 - Determine Your Value Proposition

Use what you learned in Chapter 8 to identify what your value is to this particular client. This step answers the first of The Three Magic Pre-call Questions, "Why should this client see me?"

STEP 3 - Define Your Questions

Questions help you gather information and add value. Use what you learned in Chapters 10 and 11 to determine what more you need to know in order to help this client, as well as how you can deliver value to them by asking High-Value Questions.

STEP 4 - Determine Your Advances

Use the brainstorming exercise you completed in Chapter 9 (pg. 69) to determine your Ideal Advance and Secondary Advances. Remember that they should: 1. Be specific and measurable, 2. Center on the action the prospect will take, 3. Move the sale forward, 4. Be reasonable from the prospect's perspective. After choosing your Ideal Advance and Secondary Advances, write out The Perfect Close phrase for each one. Write them verbatim so you'll be able to recall the phrasing in the heat of the moment. This step answers the second of The Three Magic Pre-call Questions, "What do I want the client to do?"

STEP 5 - Define Your Unexpected Value

Review what you learned in Chapter 10 about unexpected value and what customers value most. Then determine how you will add unexpected value on this encounter. It will likely come from one of these seven categories:

1. Deliver Insight
2. Employ Powerful Questions
3. Help Them Better Understand Their Needs
4. Help Them See the Path to Success
5. Share New Ideas
6. Deliver Education
7. Share News, Trigger Events, and Insights from Their Industry

This step answers the third of The Three Magic Pre-call Questions, "How can I provide value on this encounter?"

STEP 6 - Create Your Agenda

Use what you learned in Chapter 11 to craft an agenda. Be sure to collaborate with your client and articulate your Stated Meeting Objective. As you conduct your meeting, stick to the agenda that you and your client defined while remaining flexible. At the designated time, address the obvious action items then use The Perfect Close phrase you created for your Ideal Advance (pg. 126). If you meet with success use the Add-On variation, if not use the Fall-Back approach. Near the end of the meeting review the agreed upon action items. Cover what needs to be done, who specific tasks are assigned to, and when they will be completed. Then, establish the date and time of the next meeting.

STEP 7 - Prepare Your Mindset

Before your meeting, take advantage of the exercises and techniques you learned in Chapter 3 to ensure that your non-verbal communication sends all the right signals. Integrate your Intention Statement into your introduction or somewhere early in your meeting.

Conclusion

You now have a repeatable process for preparing for every sales encounter and advancing the sale. With a little practice it will become a habit and then you will not only become more successful, for you, success will become predictable.

EXERCISE #49 - Putting it All Together

Instructions: Select one upcoming appointment that you have not used in any of the previous exercises. Using this appointment and the accompanying forms or a blank sheet of paper walk through all seven steps you have learned.

Research Your Client (Chapter 11, Exercise 30)

Determine Your Value Proposition (Chapter 11, Exercise 31 (parts 1 and 2)

Define Your Questions (Chapter 11, Exercise 32)

Determine Your Advances (Chapter 11, Exercise 33)

Define Your Unexpected Value (Chapter 11, Exercise 34)

Create Your Agenda (Chapter 12, Exercise 37)

Prepare Your Mindset (Chapter 3)

Free Additional Resources

As a purchaser of this book you are entitled to a collection of free resources specifically designed to facilitate this learning. Download these exclusive resources at PureMuir.com/TPCworkbook using this password: Intention

The online resources include: forms for research and planning meetings, illustrations, special reports, mind maps, checklists, sample agendas, guides to make some of the exercises in the book easier, and more.

I will continue to add to these resources as time goes on. I hope you find them valuable as you continue to expand your skills and knowledge.

For your convenience in completing some of the exercises in this book, you'll find complete versions of the forms utilized in those exercises on the following pages:

- Developing Sales Objectives for every opportunity (for Exercise #13 Chapter 5)
- The Call Research Planner (for Exercise #30 Chapter 11)
- The Meeting Planner (for Exercise #37 Chapter 12)

Sales Objectives

Client/Prospect	Product /Service	Qty. & Value	Completion Date
Sales Objective ☐ Realistic			
Sales Objective ☐ Realistic			
Sales Objective ☐ Realistic			
Sales Objective ☐ Realistic			
Sales Objective ☐ Realistic			
Sales Objective ☐ Realistic			
Sales Objective ☐ Realistic			

Call Research Planner

Client Name:	
Market & Sub-Market:	
Clients: (types or named examples)	
Industry Drivers:	
Financial Status:	
Goals & Objectives:	

CURRENT SITUATION

What is the client's Current Situation & Challenges?

What is the Impact of their Current Situation & Challenges?

What hidden challenges might there be?

What might be the impact of those hidden challenges?

Which risks are likely to be of greatest concern?

ISSUES/CHALLENGES

What are the client's issues/challenges?	Impact	Priority

© James Muir - Best Practice International • www.PureMuir.com

METRICS

What metrics does the client use to measure their objective results? What are these results now? What do they want them to be? What is the value of the difference? What is the value over time?

Metric	Current Value	Desired Value	Value of Difference	Value Over Time

DECISION MAKING PROCESS

Who will be involved in the decision making process?

What process will they go through as they evaluate? Where are they at in that process now? What have they done to this point?

What is the time frame for a decision to be made? What are the drivers?

What criteria will they use to determine the ultimate solution? How will they make a decision?

What other solutions/alternatives are they or might they be considering?

OPTIONS/RESOURCES/CONSTRAINTS

What other improvement opportunities may the client be unaware of?

Who on their team will be involved in implementing the project?

Has the client given any thought to a budget for the results they are seeking?

What has kept the client from solving this problem already?

VALUE PROPOSITION / VALUE HYPOTHESIS

Why should this client see me now? What is my value hypothesis?

What tangible value can I bring to this client?

What are the metrics that measure the value I can bring?

What is the magnitude of the value I can bring?

What evidence do I have that I can help?

POSITIONING

What strengths do I bring to this opportunity?

What might the client consider to be my vulnerabilities?

QUESTIONS

	Priority
Information Questions: What additional information do I need?	
Value-Add Questions: What questions can I ask that will stimulate and facilitate my client's understanding?	

ADDITIONAL RESEARCH

What additional research do I need to conduct before my meeting?

SALES OBJECTIVE

What is my sales objective for this opportunity? *(Sales objectives should: 1. Be for a specific product/service, 2. Be Measureable (i.e. quantity), 3. Have a target date for completion, 4. Be realistic from client's perspective.)*

BRING UNEXPECTED VALUE

What unexpected value can I bring to this meeting?

Meeting Planner

Client Name:

LOGISTICS

Date: Time: Meeting Length:

Location: Contact/Meeting Coordinator:

Date Meeting Confirmed: Date Room Materials Confirmed:

Members of my team in attendance:

MEETING PURPOSE

What is the primary purpose of this meeting from your client's perspective?

What specific directive or expectations does the client have for this meeting?

ATTENDEES – Who will be in attendance? What are their meeting objectives?

Attendee	Title	Objective

OPENING COMMENTS

What will my Opening Comments be? (Will be different on initial calls vs. follow-up calls)

CREDIBILITY

What can I say / do to increase my credibility?

© James Muir – Best Practice International • www.PureMuir.com

NEW INTRODUCTIONS

What new introductions are needed? (either on the client's team or your team)

SUMMARY OF YOUR UNDERSTANDING

What is your summation of the client's current situation and challenges?

State the purpose of the current meeting:

What has changed since the last time you spoke?

Confirm timeframe if previously established. Are you still shooting for date xx/xx/xxxx?

QUESTIONS

	Priority
Information Questions: What additional information do I need?	
Value-Add Questions: What questions can I ask that will stimulate and facilitate my client's understanding?	

ISSUES/CHALLENGES

What are the client's issues/challenges? Have their priorities changed?	Impact	Priority

METRICS

What metrics does the client use to measure their objective results? What are these results now? What do they want them to be? What is the value of the difference? What is the value over time?

Metric	Current Value	Desired Value	Value of Difference	Value Over Time

VALUE PROPOSITION / VALUE HYPOTHESIS

Why should this client see me now? What is my value hypothesis?

What tangible value can I bring to this client?

What are the metrics that measure the value I can bring?

What is the magnitude of the value I can bring?

What evidence do I have that I can help?

POSITIONING

What strengths do I bring to this opportunity?

What might the client consider to be my vulnerabilities?

CALL OBJECTIVES / ADVANCES

What is my primary call objective? (*Call Objectives should be: 1. Specific & measurable, 2. Center on the action the client will take, 3. Move the sale forward, 4. Be reasonable from the client's perspective*)

What is my Ideal Advance for this meeting?

Perfect Close phrase:

SECONDARY / BACKUP OBJECTIVES

What are my secondary/backup objectives?

-
-
-

What are my alternate/additional Advances for this meeting?

-
-
-

Perfect Close phrases:

-
-
-

MINIMUM ADVANCE

What is the smallest advance I am willing to accept and still move forward?

Perfect Close phrase:

BRING UNEXPECTED VALUE

What unexpected value can I bring to this meeting?

James Muir

Recommended Reading

As a voracious consumer of books, I am frequently asked to recommend sales books. Here are some of my favorites in the area of sales and sales management.

Sales

7L: The Seven Levels of Communication: Go from Relationships to Referrals - Michael Maher
Achieve Sales Excellence: The 7 Customer Rules for Becoming the New Sales Professional - Howard Stevens, Theodore Kinni
Adapt or Fail: Process with Power - Michael Nick
Agile Selling: Get Up to Speed Quickly in Today's Ever-Changing Sales World - Jill Konrath
Amp Up Your Sales: Powerful Strategies That Move Customers to Make Fast, Favorable Decisions - Andy Paul
Be Bold and Win the Sale: Get Out of Your Comfort Zone and Boost Your Performance - Jeff Shore
Bottom-Line Selling: The Sales Professional's Guide to Improving Customer Profits - Jack Malcolm
Building a StoryBrand: Clarify Your Message So Customers Will Listen - Donald Miller
Combo Prospecting: The Powerful One-Two Punch That Fills Your Pipeline and Wins Sales - Tony J. Hughes
Consultative Selling: The Hanan Formula for High-Margin Sales at High Levels - Mack Hanan
Dealstorming: The Secret Weapon That Can Solve Your Toughest Sales Challenges - Tim Sanders
DISCOVER Questions Get You Connected: For Professional Sellers - Deb Calvert
Do YOU Mean Business? Technical/Non-Technical Collaboration, Business Development and YOU - Babette N. Ten Haken
Eat Their Lunch: Winning Customers Away from Your Competition - Anthony Iannarino
EDGY Conversations: How Ordinary People Can Achieve Outrageous Success - Dan Waldschmidt
Emotional Intelligence for Sales Success: Connect with Customers and Get Results - Colleen Stanley
Endless Referrals - Bob Burg
Escaping the Price-Driven Sale: How World Class Sellers Create Extraordinary Profit - Tom Snyder, Kevin Kearns
Fanatical Prospecting: The Ultimate Guide to Opening Sales Conversations and Filling the Pipeline by Leveraging Social Selling, Telephone, Email, Text, and Cold Calling - Jeb Blount
Go for No! Yes is the Destination, No is How You Get There - Richard Fenton, Andrea Waltz
Go-Givers Sell More - Bob Burg
High-Profit Prospecting: Powerful Strategies to Find the Best Leads and Drive Breakthrough Sales Results - Mark Hunter
High-Profit Selling: Win the Sale Without Compromising on Price - Mark Hunter
How I Raised Myself from Failure to Success in Selling - Frank Bettger
How to Become a Rainmaker: The Rules for Getting and Keeping Customers and Clients - Jeffery J. Fox
How to Get a Meeting with Anyone: The Untapped Selling Power of Contact Marketing - Stu Heinecke
How to Win Friends and Influence People - Dale Carnegie
Influence: Science and Practice - Robert B. Cialdini
Insight Selling: Surprising Research on What Sales Winners Do Differently - Mike Schultz, John E. Doerr
Integrity Selling for the 21st Century: How to Sell the Way People Want to Buy - Ron Willingham
Jeffrey Gitomer's Little Red Book of Selling: 12.5 Principles for Sales Greatness: How to Make Sales FOREVER - Jeffrey Gitomer
Lead, Sell, or Get Out of the Way: The 7 Traits of Great Sellers - Ron Karr
Let's Get Real or Let's Not Play: Transforming the Buyer/Seller Relationship - Mahan Khalsa
Love Is the Killer App: How to Win Business and Influence Friends - Tim Sanders
Mastering the Complex Sale - Jeff Thull
Never Be Closing: How to Sell Better Without Screwing Your Clients, Your Colleagues, or Yourself - Tim Hurson
New Sales. Simplified. The Essential Handbook for Prospecting and New Business Development - Mike Weinberg
Nice Girls DO Get the Sale: Relationship Building That Gets Results - Elinor Stutz
No More Cold Calling: The Breakthrough System That Will Leave Your Competition in the Dust - Joanne S. Black
Objections: The Ultimate Guide for Mastering the Art and Science of Getting Past No - Jeb Blount
Perfect Selling - Linda Richardson
Perpetual Hunger: Sales Prospecting Lessons & Strategy - Patrick Tinney
Pitch Anything: An Innovative Method for Presenting, Persuading, and Winning the Deal - Oren Klaff
Power Phone Scripts: 500 Word-for-Word Questions, Phrases, and Conversations to Open and Close More Sales - Mike Brooks
Predictable Revenue: Turn Your Business Into a Sales Machine with the $100 Million Best Practices of Salesforce.com - Aaron Ross
Pick Up the Damn Phone! How People, Not Technology, Seal the Deal - Joanne S. Black
Questions that Sell: The Powerful Process for Discovering What Your Customer Really Wants - Paul Cherry
Quit Whining and Start Selling! A Step-by-Step Guide to a Hall of Fame Career in Sales - Kelly S. Riggs
Rainmaking Conversations: Influence, Persuade, and Sell in Any Situation - Mike Schultz, John E. Doerr
ROI Selling: Increasing Revenue, Profit, and Customer Loyalty through the 360 Sales Cycle - Michael Nick

Sales Chaos: Using Agility Selling to Think and Sell Differently - Tim Ohai
Sales Differentiation: 19 Powerful Strategies to Win More Deals at the Prices You Want - Lee Salz
Sales EQ: How Ultra High Performers Leverage Sales-Specific Emotional Intelligence to Close the Complex Deal - Jeb Blount
Screen to Selling: How to Increase Sales, Productivity, and Customer Experience with the Latest Technology - Doug Devitre
Selling Against the Goal: How Corporate Sales Professionals Generate the Leads They Need - Kendra Lee
Selling Fearlessly: A Master Salesman's Secrets for The One-Call-Close Salesperson - Robert Terson
Selling from The Heart: How Your Authentic Self Sells You! - Larry Levine
Selling to Big Companies - Jill Konrath
Selling to the C-Suite: What Every Executive Wants You to Know About Successfully Selling to the Top - Stephen J. Bistritz, Nicholas A.C. Read
Seven Stories Every Salesperson Must Tell - Mike Adams
Shift! Harness the Trigger Events That Turn Prospects Into Customers - Craig Elias, Tibor Shanto
Six Secrets of Sales Magnets: Learn What the TOP 5% of All Salespeople Do and How YOU Can Do It Too - Laura Posey
Smart Calling: Eliminate the Fear, Failure, and Rejection from Cold Calling - Art Sobczak
SNAP Selling: Speed Up Sales and Win More Business with Today's Frazzled Customers - Jill Konrath
SPIN Selling - Neil Rackham
Stop Selling and Start Leading: How to Make Extraordinary Sales Happen - Deb Calvert, James Kouzes, Barry Posner
Strategic Sales Presentations - Jack Malcolm
Swim with the Sharks Without Being Eaten Alive - Harvey Mackay
Take the Cold Out of Cold Calling - Sam Richter
The 25 Sales Habits of Highly Successful Salespeople - Stephen Schiffman
The 7 Habits of Highly Effective People: Powerful Lessons in Personal Change - Stephen R. Covey
The Challenger Customer: Selling to the Hidden Influencer Who Can Multiply Your Results - Brent Adamson, Matthew Dixon, Pat Spenner, Nick Toman
The Art of Commercial Conversations: When It's Your Turn to Make A Difference - Bernadette McClelland
The Challenger Sale: Taking Control of the Customer Conversation - Matthew Dixon, Brent Adamson
The Go-Giver, Expanded Edition: A Little Story About a Powerful Business Idea - Bob Burg, John David Mann
The Greatest Salesman in the World - Og Mandino
The Introvert's Edge: How the Quiet and Shy Can Outsell Anyone - Matthew Pollard
The Lost Art of Closing: Winning the Ten Commitments That Drive Sales - Anthony Iannarino
The Miracle Morning for Salespeople: The Fastest Way to Take Your SELF and Your SALES to the Next Level - Hal Elrod
The New Strategic Selling: The Unique Sales System Proven Successful by the World's Best Companies - Robert B. Miller, Stephen E. Heiman, Tad Tuleja
The No. 1 Best Seller: A Unique Insight Into the Mind, Strategy and Processes of a Top Salesman - Lee Bartlett
The Only Sales Guide You'll Ever Need - Anthony Iannarino
The Psychology of Selling: Increase Your Sales Faster and Easier Than You Ever Thought Possible - Brian Tracy
The Sales Magnet: How to Get More Customers Without Cold Calling - Kendra Lee
The Science of Selling: Proven Strategies to Make Your Pitch, Influence Decisions, and Close the Deal - David Hoffeld
The SPIN Selling Fieldbook: Practical Tools, Methods, Exercises, and Resources - Neil Rackham
Think and Grow Rich - Napoleon Hill
Think Like Your Customer: A Winning Strategy to Maximize Sales by Understanding and Influencing How and Why Your Customers Buy - Bill Stinnet
To Sell Is Human: The Surprising Truth About Moving Others - Daniel H. Pink
Trust-Based Selling: Using Customer Focus and Collaboration to Build Long-Term Relationships - Charles H. Green
Unlimited Selling Power: How to Master Hypnotic Skills - Donald Moine
Unlocking Yes: Sales Negotiation Lessons & Strategy - Patrick Tinney
Whale Hunting: How to Land Big Sales and Transform Your Company - Tom Searcy, Barbara Weaver Smith

Sales Management
Awesomely Simple: Essential Business Strategies for Turning Ideas Into Action - John Spence
Coaching Salespeople Into Sales Champions: A Tactical Playbook for Managers and Executives - Keith Rosen
Cracking the Sales Management Code: The Secrets to Measuring and Managing Sales Performance - Jason Jordan, Michelle Vazzana
Predictable Revenue: Turn Your Business Into A Sales Machine With the $100 Million Best Practices of Salesforce.com - Aaron Ross
Sales Management Simplified: The Straight Truth About Getting Exceptional Results from Your Sales Team - Mike Weinberg
Sales Manager Survival Guide: Lessons from Sales' Front Lines - David Brock
Smarketing: How to Achieve Competitive Advantage through Blended Sales and Marketing - Tim Hughes
The Sales Acceleration Formula: Using Data, Technology, and Inbound Selling to Go from $0 to $100 Million - Mark Roberge
The Sales Development Playbook: Build Repeatable Pipeline and Accelerate Growth with Inside Sales - Trish Bertuzzi
The Sales Manager's Guide to Greatness: 10 Essential Strategies for Leading Your Team to the Top - Kevin F. Davis
The Ultimate Sales Machine: Turbocharge Your Business with Relentless Focus on 12 Key Strategies - Chet Holmes
Your Sales Management Guru's Guide to… Leading High-Performance Sales Teams - Ken Thoreson

Request For Review

I sincerely hope you have enjoyed and benefited from this workbook. I am on a mission to take the dysfunction out of sales and teach sales and service professionals how being genuinely authentic creates the highest levels of success and happiness.

Please help others to learn more about how they can improve their approach to closing. The best way is simply to share it with your friends and colleagues. There's another way we can reach even more people. If you write a simple review on Amazon, you can help hundreds, or perhaps even thousands, of readers to make a buying decision that will improve their lives. Like you, they work hard for every penny they spend on books. With your feedback and encouragement, you can help them focus on the right things and take immediate action.

In your review share anything you think will be useful to others. Here are a few suggestions:
- Why did you decide to get this workbook?
- What did you like most about the workbook?
- What makes this workbook different from others you have experienced?
- Did it give you practical ways to apply the info it provides? If so, share what you will do differently now that you have this knowledge.
- What readers do you think would benefit most from this workbook?

The best time to write a review is immediately after you've read the book while everything is still fresh in your mind. Please head over to Amazon.com and write a quick review right now.

About the Author

James Muir is the author of the best-selling book, *The Perfect Close: The Secret to Closing Sales*, which reveals practices and techniques to help sales and service professionals close the deal using a clear, practical, and comfortable approach that will increase their number of closed opportunities and accelerate their sales to the highest levels – all while remaining genuinely, authentic.

James is a professional speaker, author, sales trainer, and coach. He shattered records as both a field rep and manager. His guidance comes from the school of hard knocks. Three decades of experience has given James a fresh and practical perspective on what works in real life and what doesn't.

James has an extensive background in healthcare technology sales where he has sold and spoken to the largest names in healthcare and technology including HCA, Tenet, Catholic Healthcare, Banner, Dell, IBM, and others.

Focused on helping individuals and teams improve and streamline their business practices, James covers a variety of today's most important topics, including: closing, productivity, management, prospecting, sales strategies, motivation, and authentic sales skills.

Those interested in learning more can reach him at PureMuir.com.

Contact Info
Phone: 801-633-4444
Website: PureMuir.com
Email: jmuir @ PureMuir.com
LinkedIn: https://www.linkedin.com/in/puremuir
Twitter: @B2B_SalesTips

Made in the USA
Middletown, DE
16 September 2022

10536051R00091